Castle Park

Castle Park

Sam Hair

CREATIVE ARTS BOOK COMPANY
Berkeley California

Copyright © 2000 by Sam Hair

No part of this book may be reproduced in any manner
without the written permission of the publisher,
except in brief quotations used in articles or reviews.

For information contact:
Creative Arts Book Company
833 Bancroft Way
Berkeley, California 94710
www.creativeartsbooks.com

ISBN 0-88739-460-4

Printed in the United States of America

I. Castle Park   *1*

II. Clifton   *48*

III. Rocky Mountain National Park   *54*

IV. The University   *77*

V. The Rock   *100*

VI. Finis Origine Pendet   *129*

Castle Park Tournament

Aquatic Carnival
Saturday, August 23, 1919
MORNING EVENTS
10:00 a. m. to 12:00 m.

Judges
E. N. ACKERMAN
CHAS. R. MURRAY
W. J. REYNOLDS

Referee
H. W. SPURRIER
Aquatic Coach, Chicago Athletic Association
Starter
CARTER P. BROWN
Timer
DR. FRANK W. JAY

1 **Children's Tug of War**—Teams to be drawn on the beach.

2 **Women's Tug of War**—Teams to be drawn on the beach.

3 **Boys' Swimming Race**—Handicap, under fifteen years.
Contestants—(1) Bruce Hulbert, (2) John Fuqua, (3) Robert Ackerman, (4) Edward Post, (5) Chas. Orton, (6) Frederick Goff, (7) Thomas Hair, Jr., (8) George Paul, (9) Louis Volkma, (10) Carl Lundberg, (11) Rowland Howe, (12) Perry Owens, (13) Ray Orton, (14) Gordon Murray, (15) Kenneth Peirce.
Winners:
1................2................3................

4 **Canoe Bow Race**—Distance, one-fourth mile—all ages.
Contestants—(16) Lowell Hall, (17) Philo Orton, (18) Julius Goeble, (19) Dick Goeble, (15) Kenneth Peirce, (20) Phil Jewell, (21) "Commie" Johnson.

5 **Girls' Swimming Race** — Handicap, under fifteen years.
Contestants—(22) Betty Thornton, (23) Barbara Ackerman, (24) "Buddy" Beach, (25) Hortense Fuqua, (26) Dorothy Jay, (27) Marion Jay, (28) Majorie van Benschoten, (29) Catherine Howe, (30) Frances Green.
Winners:
1................2................3................

6 **Jumping Canoe Race**—Open contest—free for all.

7 **Girls' Obstacle Race**—Free for all—under fifteen years.
Stunt—From line on beach to sand bar around boat or buoy, back to diving pier, up over same returning to starting point.
Contestants—(31) Frances Waddell, (32) Eunice Goeble, (33) Bunt Goeble, (34) Lynette Brown, (35) Helen Goodell, (27) Marion Jay, (36) Ruth van Benschoten, (37) Helen Goff, (38) Hazel Robertson, (39) Caroline Parker, (40) Louise Smith, (41) Helen Richardson, (42) Mazie Vance, (43) Dorothy Vance.
Winners:
1................2................3................

EXTRA SPECIAL EVENT!

Fancy Diving Exhibition . . . . by Captain Bill Stahl
Swan Dive, Front Jack-Knife, Back Jack-Knife, Full Flying Dutchman, Running 1½ Somersault, Standing 1½ Somersault, Front Jack-Knife with half twist and other dives.

LUNCHEON AT THE CASTLE
(in bathing attire only)

AFTERNOON EVENTS
1:45 p. m. to 4:00 p. m.

SPECIAL EVENT!—Challenge Swimming Match
Distance ⅛ mile
Contestants (63) Mrs. Helen R. Miller vs. (35) Helen Goodell
Winner................................

8 **Canoe Tilting**—Blues vs. Reds.
BLUES   **REDS**
(17) Philo Orton (14) Gordon Murray (19) Dick Goebel (13) Ray Orton
(44) Billy van Ben (45) Bill Stahl (46) Ralph Pierson (20) Phil Jewell
(18) Julius Goebel (47) Van Ellis (16) Lowell Hall (15) Kenneth Peirce
(48) Robert Craig and (49) "Mich" Peirce, Alternates
Winners................................

9 **Diving Contest**—
Contestants—(1) Bruce Hulbert, (50) Eldredge Murray, (33) "Bunt" Goeble, (19) Dick Goeble, (51) Doctor Jay, (27) Marion Jay, (52) Edward Tanner, (53) Frank Dimond.
Winners:
1................2................3................

A Most Interesting and Instructive Event
Demonstration of Life Saving
H. W. SPURRIER
Diploma Holder Royal Life Saving Society
Winner of Kings Cup 1908-9-10

10 **Grand Canoe Race**—Distance, two miles.
LAVENDER
(17) Philo Orton, (14) Gordon Murray, (37) Helen Goff
BLUE
(44) Bill van Ben, (45) Bill Stahl (32) Eunice Goebel
ORANGE
(18) Julius Goebel (47) Van Ellis (34) Lynette Brown
GREEN
(19) Dick Goebel (13) Ray Orton (38) Hazel Robertson
RED
(46) Ralph Pierson (20) Phil Jewell (42) Mazie Vance
WHITE
(15) Kenneth Peirce (16) Lowell Hall (31) Frances Waddell
YELLOW
(48) Robert Craig (49) "Mich" Peirce (36) Ruth van Benschoten
1................2................3................

I. CASTLE PARK

It was a haven for tired fathers from Chicago who took "the boat," the Pere Marquette train, or drove the 145 miles up US-31 and M-11 to Saugatuck, and then the asphalt single-lane road, partly paralleling the interurban tracks. Driving into the Castle there was a grade coming around from the dirt road which left M-11 at Grafschaap. In the 1920s with a load of children, dogs and summer equipage, one had to shift gears to get up this slight hill before coming around the bend in the road and then downhill to the Castle.

This trip took two days. For us, the first day from the south side of Chicago ended at the Whitcomb Hotel in St. Joseph, Michigan, a twin city to Benton Harbor. We had two large rooms on the third floor, three children and the dog in one room, the parents in the other. Up early the next morning to get into the Buick touring car and go the remaining seventy-five miles of mostly dirt roads along the east side of Lake Michigan—South Haven, Coloma, Watervliet, Paw Paw Lake, Glenn, Douglas. When we got to Saugatuck and the last fourteen miles, we knew were almost there.

The only entrance to Castle Park was via the dirt road between Saugatuck and Macatawa that veered sharply off the main paved road. The Castle was, and still is, a four-story yellow brick building that looks like a castle because it has battlements all around the roof and a round tower higher than the roof at one corner with small windows at every landing of the inside staircase. It functioned as a hotel, post office, and soda fountain and contained the only telephone—a hand cranked one—in the Castle office. There were no other telephones at Castle Park, nor was there any electricity. The Castle did have a noisy old stationary engine in the back to run a generator that furnished enough power to light up the various rooms. It was turned off at eleven o'clock every night, at which time kerosene lamps placed in every room were used. The engine was turned off because it would have kept everybody in the hotel awake as well as those in nearby cottages.

The Castle was owned by the Parr family originally, then purchased by Mr. Donald Wilkie in 1915. When Carter Brown graduated from the University of Illinois in 1916, he married Mr. Wilkie's daughter Marion, and became a partner in the firm of Brown & Wilkie. Mr. Wilkie was getting on in years and gave over the whole management responsibility to Carter. Their property included not only the Castle but several nearby cottages and a couple of acres behind the Castle where there was the sheltered parking area, the stable, and the dormitory for the waiters, known as "The Shack." The golf course, the water supply pumping station, and much of the beachfront area were owned by the Castle Park Association, of which every cottage owner was a member.

Carter Brown turned out to be a talented outdoorsman, amateur architect, and skilled horseman. He was a non-smoker and non-drinker, but tolerant of others who had dissimilar habits. He was dedicated to Castle Park and everything in it. He was able, maybe without knowing it, to establish the collegial atmosphere of Castle Park by listening patiently to all who came with a problem or a situation that needed attention and dealing with it himself if he could, even if he had no authority to do so. Sometimes he had to call a meeting of the people involved and the directors of the Castle Park Association were happy to have him do this so that they wouldn't have to deal with problems themselves. No conflict among the property owners remained unresolved for very long. Carter knew that Castle Park was an exclusive resort and people didn't come there to get into stressful situations. One had to be a property owner, a renter of a cottage, or a guest in the hotel and to be any of those, you had to be recommended by a member of the association.

Another Brown & Wilkie property was the Pine Crest Inn in Tryon, North Carolina. The Castle Park season was from June through September. In early October the Castle would close, the horses in the stable would be sent back to Tryon, and Carter Brown would be gone until the following June to run the hotel and riding stable there.

Sometimes telegrams were telephoned to the Castle for delivery to a particular cottage. Carter Brown had a megaphone and when a telegram came in he would go to the front steps of the Castle and announce it in his loud baritone voice, "Telegram! Telegram! For Doctor Vance!" or whoever might be the addressee, repeated several times. Whenever one of us boys heard this, we would rush over to pick up the typewritten telegram on the yellow Western Union form and run with it to the appropriate cottage. This was rewarded with a dime or sometimes even a quarter. One of those messages that we heard about in 1920 was carried by Carter Brown himself. It told of the death in a hospital in France of a Castle Park family member, a casualty of World War I. Most of these messages told of the arrival time of those who needed to be met at the Pere Marquette train in Holland or the overnight boat from Chicago that came to Macatawa.

CASTLE PARK IN THE 1920s

My father bought our cottage from Mr. Ackerman in 1920. It was called "Pine Knoll" and it was the last cottage in a row of three near South Hill behind the Castle. It was reached by a steep series of steps from the road that went to the amphitheater. Consequently, it was somewhat isolated and hauling anything heavy up those steps was difficult. It was isolated also from the activity centered around the cottages overlooking the lake and closer to the Castle, but I liked our cottage anyway. The front door opened on to the second floor, up a few steps from another side door entrance below and to the right. On the second floor there were four bedrooms and a bath. The Kitchen and dining room were beneath on the first floor with the master bedroom and bath and an open porch for eating or sleeping. From the second floor, there were steps leading up to my brother Tom's bedroom on the third floor. I was given the back bedroom on the second floor.

The windows remained open most of the time in the summer. When I was lying in bed in the morning, I could hear all that was happening at the stable area behind the Castle. The old Model T Ford flatbed truck there was used to haul ice from the icehouse to the Castle Park iceboxes. This truck had to be cranked and its four-cylinder engine made a loud putt-putting noise when it started. Carter Brown often swore at it, using words he thought no one would hear. The ice was cut every winter from nearby Kelly Lake, sawed into large blocks and stored under a thick blanket of sawdust in a dark barn next to the stable.

I was sent to bed at nine o'clock each night when the Castle twice-a-week dance was just beginning. On those quiet, warm nights with my bedroom window open, I could hear the music almost as if I were there on the dance floor. To this day, when I hear the popular songs of the 1920s, I'm brought back to summer nights when I was too little to be up, like the child in Robert Louis Stevenson's "Bed In Summer." The dances were every Wednesday and Saturday night at the Castle in the big sun parlor off the main lobby, a sort of oval-shaped room with many windows. Herb Van Duren and his band came to the Castle on these nights during July and August for several years in the 20s. He would begin playing at nine P.M. and continue until eleven. Then he would pack up everything in two cars and drive as fast as he could to South Haven, about forty miles south, down the shore of Lake Michigan on highway M-11 from Saugatuck, where he would play from midnight to two A.M. in a nightclub there on the lakefront.

He had other weeknight engagements, but his Wednesdays and Saturdays were probably his busiest. He and his group sat at one end of the sun parlor, with the drummer and piano player in back and the banjo and saxophone in front with Herb who played the trumpet and did the vocals.

I first heard Herb in 1920 when I was five and put to bed at nine o'clock in the evening. Later, when I was ten, I could stay up until ten. There was a window bench behind the piano and when the music started at nine I would be there, very quiet and unobtrusive, and the piano player, Keats Dumont, didn't care as long as I didn't bother him. My proximity to the music made it almost deafening, but I was transfixed at being so close and unseen. I sat there the whole hour from nine to ten before I had to go up to our cottage and to bed.

Prohibition was in effect then, but it didn't make any difference to our family because my father would never permit alcohol or tobacco in our house anyway, and nobody at Castle Park openly drank much that I remember. There were no bootleggers in the area that we ever heard about. Occasionally, the Castle Park people from Detroit would bring in whisky from across the river in Windsor, Ontario. Carter Brown, the owner of the Castle, was positive in his insistence that the Castle Park Association prohibit any alcoholic beverages in any form from being served by anybody anywhere on the association's grounds. This included the cottages, the golf course, the beach, the waterworks, and the hotel. I'm sure that some of the cottage owners served cocktails whenever they wanted to, but always with great circumspection and respect for Carter Brown by keeping quiet about it.

THE BEACH

An announcement program of a water carnival at Castle Park in 1919 shows the collegial atmosphere of those times shortly after the First World War. Since I was only four-years-old then, I have no real recollection of that day. My brother Tom's name appears as an entry in the swimming race for boys under fifteen. He was then ten. Almost all of the families I remember from later summers were participants. At the time, and for the next thirty years until the 1950s, the beach on Lake Michigan was a wide strip of clean sand about 200 feet from the water to the dunes. In the late 50s, it became apparent that the water level of the Great Lakes was rising enough to take away the Castle Park beach. The water came to the dune so now there is swimming in the lake in the summertime, but the many hours spent on the beach in years gone by came to an end. This has changed the character of Castle Park because the beach, in the afternoons of mid-June to Labor Day, was for many years the social center for the whole community. Pre-school kids up to teenagers ready to go to college were on the beach together with their parents, friends, and dogs. Boys learned what girls looked like in bathing suits as they grew up, and girls learned how to deal with the boys who were finding this out.

There were two diving platforms, one about two feet off the water and close to shore, the other about eight feet off the deeper water offshore with a real springboard. A dozen or so boys and girls could congregate on these and dive and splash and play in the water. Early one summer I managed to retrieve a damaged canoe that had been abandoned and left all winter on the beach. Half of it was still intact and I took some of the outer canvas from the other half and made a sort-of jerry-built half-canoe that would hold two sitting in its bottom. Ted DeBoer helped me do this on a couple of afternoons. When it was done, he said we would have to christen it. He found a can of white paint in the trunk of his Duesenberg and said, "All right, Sam, let's name it *The Frantic*. I was so impressed with this that I could only nod my head and let him do it. So he painted the name in large block letters on the canvas stern of my half-canoe. When the summer was over, I abandoned this vessel as my father said we had no place to put it away and save it. The following summer I could find no trace of it. It did not survive another winter on the beach.

"PROF" TAYLOR

We had all been taught to swim by "The Professor," as he called himself, so we all called him "Prof." For twenty years he was a denizen of Castle Park, first as a swimming teacher of small children just beginning to venture into the friendly summer waters of Lake Michigan. He was heavily handsome, burly, and tall, uneducated, but with a firm authoritative manner and positive opinions. Somehow, he knew how to gain the confidence of the parents so that they entrusted their children to his somewhat heavy-handed ministrations in the water.

The Professor had his own method of teaching: He had an arrangement of canvas straps attached around a child floating face down in the water with the Prof exhorting him loudly, "Open up them eyes!" and "Paddle with your feet!" He taught us how to get our faces out of the water and breathe in and put our faces down in the water and breathe out as we were suspended by the canvas straps around our midriffs. He would teach us the side-stroke and the breast-stroke, but never the crawl. He said all he wanted to do was to teach us to swim in water that was over our heads so we wouldn't drown.

When he thought one of us was ready to do this, he would take the child and his father out off the beach in a canoe into deeper water and the boy would jump out of the canoe and swim ashore about fifty feet unassisted by the Prof, who followed behind. This was an important rite of passage for us and was as good a way as any to give us confidence in the water at an early age. Dozens of Castle Park kids later included in their memories of boyhood days at the beach the Prof who taught them to swim.

After some years as a swimming teacher, he opened a small restaurant about two miles out on the road to Holland near what was then a neighborhood called Central Park. It was clean and bright with a counter and four booths in shades of gray and blue and had a limited menu.

From his soda fountain you could get a "brown cow" or a "black cow", large mugs filled with a mixture of ice cream and root beer or Coca-Cola. He also heartily recommended his Vernor's Ginger Ale, which was his exclusively in that neighborhood. The main specialty was his hamburgers and cheeseburgers, which he made himself from choice ground steak. They were generous and served on Holland Rusks with lettuce and tomatoes. He got a good price for them and we knew that the Professor's hamburgers were as he described them, the best.

For the first two years in this business he worked early and late. He was the cook and the waiter. He would take our orders and shout them over his shoulder to someone in the kitchen, then run back and cook the orders because there wasn't anybody in the kitchen. After several years, we came to Castle Park one summer to find that Prof Taylor's place had been taken over by someone else and we never saw him again. The place was not the same and we didn't go there any more. We heard that he had gone to Detroit to work in a factory.

1919–Sam Hair, Eleanor Hair, Tom Hair, "Prof" Taylor

SIR JOSH

In the tower of the Castle, with an entrance from the roof, was an artist's studio occupied for many years by Wellington Reynolds, a Chicago artist. Carter Brown gave him the space up there and he occupied one of the rooms in the hotel part of the Castle. Early on, he was called "Sir Josh" after the eminent British painter, Sir Joshua Reynolds. He didn't seem to mind and may even have thought it flattery.

Above the Castle on the way to South Hill on the left side of the road through the trees was a ravine with a steep slope from the road to a flat area of about a half-acre at the base of the slope, overgrown with small trees and shrubbery. Sir Josh persuaded the Castle Park Association to raise money for the construction of a Greek Amphitheater with seats on the slope and the stage at its base, set back with an open area in front. It was agreed that this particular location lent itself to the idea as it would require no excavation but only clearing out the area for the seats and the stage. Sir Josh supervised all this, which went on for about four summers. He won some respect for a certain authenticity, which he insisted on, but which those involved in the actual building thought strange, if not unnecessary. There were stone busts of Sophocles and Euripides on pillars at the top of the stairs going down through the seating area. The seats were formed by terraces in a broad half-circle in front of the open area before the stage. Most people brought pillows to sit on. There was a life-size statue of Hebe at stage rear, which could be hidden by a drop cloth if she got in the way of a stage production. The backdrop of the stage was the tree-covered hillside that formed the other side of the ravine. At either side of the stage was an enclosed area with an outside wall facing the audience. On each of the walls was painted a mask of comedy on one side and tragedy on the other. In these enclosures were stored an upright piano, the hymn books for the vespers services, and a few other items which might be used for any outdoor theatrical production. The stage had no curtain because Sir Josh said Greek amphitheaters did not have them.

Sunday evenings at five o'clock there was a vespers service with a preacher from Holland coming out to give a sermon. Most of these ministers were of a Dutch Reform persuasion, as that's about all Holland, Michigan, has, but the Castle Park vespers services were non- denominational with a few hymns, a sermon, and the passing of a collection plate. Music for the hymns was furnished by the piano, played vigorously by Mildred Peirce and accompanied by Grace Holverscheid who would lead the singing with her accomplished mezzo soprano voice. The amphitheater acquired a degree of renown among architects and classical scholars because it did resemble, on a smaller scale, such ancient outdoor theaters as Epidaurus.

When Sir Josh was not working on the building of the amphitheater of helping to take care of it after it was built, he was producing large numbers of oil paintings of his favorite subjects: Lake Michigan sunrises, sunsets and beaches. Winters he could be found at his studio on East 57th Street in Chicago near the university. There he did portraits mostly and was quite successful at it, being called upon to do many for various important people in Chicago, especially in the university area. Summers at the Castle he would stride down to the beach daily after breakfast and again after lunch. Wearing a long bathrobe over his bathing suit and a pith helmet, suitable for those living in British Africa, he carried in both arms his easel, canvases, palette, and box of paints. We never saw his studio in the tower as he did not encourage children or any others to visit him there and he largely ignored us. It was clear he was a serious artist and not to be trifled with.

HAROLD TIBBE

Kelly Lake was a small body of shallow water just outside the Castle grounds beyond the interurban tracks and south of the road to Graafschap. Mr. Tibbe and his family lived at the far edge of the lake where he had a small farm on which he raised some corn, hay, and a few vegetables and berries. In the summer season, he had a little roadside stand where the farm produce was offered for sale. Driving out from the Castle we could see only one side of his farmhouse, which was always covered with tarpaper, making it appear to be unfinished. Each year when we first arrived to spend the summer at the Castle, the Tibbe house, with its tarpaper exposure, remained unchanged. Mrs. Tibbe, a large, tired-looking woman, did laundry for the Castle Park mothers who would bring it to her at the farmhouse. She told my mother that her husband was working on an addition to the house, but for over ten years we could see no such work going on and I don't believe it was ever finished.

We seldom saw Mr. Tibbe, he was always out in the fields, and I never once saw him on my visits to Kelly Lake where we would go occasionally to fish from its banks for sunfish and perch. Their daughter Mae was a young teenager, quite pretty and soft-spoken and polite to all the summer people. She was available for baby-sitting and sometimes helped with light cleaning of the cottages. She was off-limits for the boys at Castle Park, and went immediately home when her work at any of the cottages was done.

The son, Harold Tibbe, was a figure of some mystery and romance, although we never saw him at all. This was because he was in the Michigan State Prison at Ionia. It seems that Sheriff Van Noss had surprised Harold one winter when most of the cottages were deserted and Harold was inside one of the more luxurious lake-front houses, about to carry off an outboard motor and two rifles. The sheriff, a neighbor and friend of the Tibbe family, reluctantly did his duty and Harold ended up in Ionia. It was the second time around for Harold. He had had a previous conviction on the same charge but had received a suspended sentence then because he had no record. His act of breaking and entering was attributed to a youthful indiscretion not likely to happen again. The word "Ionia" had a touch of glamour about it because we didn't really know anybody who had actually gone to prison. We felt that we knew Harold Tibbe, a neighbor whom we never saw but who was somehow a fearless adventurer and dared to do things we would never do. Those who knew him before he fell from virtue described him as a handsome young man who was a star athlete at the local high school, but was unable to resist the temptation of all those deserted Castle Park cottages full of things he thought he had to have. In later years, I never found out what happened to Harold. I hope that, like Raskolnikov, his punishment was his redemption.

TED DEBOER

Ted DeBoer was a waiter at Castle Park for only two summers as he was much too energetic and entrepreneurial to do what he called "college-boy stuff" work. He was always polite and good-natured and got along fine with the other waiters and the guests at the Castle. Ted surprised us sometimes with his abilities to do things that no one had any idea he could do. To us younger pre-teen boys he was romantic, heroic, handsome, mysterious, and dashing because he arrived one summer, driving a Duesenberg, ready to start work at the Castle.

It was his very own 1925 Duesenberg touring car, somewhat beat-up but still magnificent. In his spare time he was frequently seen either under the car doing something to it or with his head under the raised hood working on the engine. He had disconnected the tail-pipe so that the huge straight-eight engine would produce a real racket when he took off, kicking up dirt and gravel with the rear wheels spinning. We were fascinated as he drove out of the parking lot at the rear of the Castle, engine roaring and dirt flying, with his aviator glasses on and his hair blowing in the wind.

He knew that we were all wanting him to give us a ride anywhere, anytime, just to be in that car. He waited for about a month until he had it cleaned up, had put on two new side-mount tires, and had finished the valve job he was working on., Then, one afternoon when he saw me on the way to the beach, he said, "Hey, Sam, come on. We'll go to Macatawa. Be back in a little while." I rode beside him in the front seat and was silently entranced with this long-sought privilege: the ride in the Duesenberg. The road to Macatawa was dirt with bumpy washboard intervals, never adequately graded and maintained by the county, but the Duesenberg roared right along at sixty miles an hour, making a large satisfying noise. Ted was on an errand for Carter Brown so he only went to the post office and then returned. He let me out at the Castle and I raced to the beach to tell my friends I had ridden in the Duesenberg. At various times later that summer, Ted took me on rides to Holland and back.

Later that summer, Ted surprised everyone at one of the dances at the Castle. He had a date with Barbara Hall, another shy, gently brought up, eighteen-year-old daughter of one of the old Castle Park families who had been spending summers there for many years. It was accepted custom for the waiters at the Castle dining room to ask these girls to go with them only to the dances. They never asked the girls to go to Holland, to the movies, to Saugatuck to the Big Pavilion, or anywhere else outside the Castle grounds. At eleven o'clock, the girl and her waiter date would walk back to her cottage and that was the end of the evening. No waiter was ever invited in to sit a while and chat. It was "good night" at the front door, indicative of the barrier between the waiters and the girls of the Castle Park families.

Ted DeBoer was very casual with these girls, keeping as much distance from each one as she was supposed to stay away from him, emotionally speaking. The barrier was as much his as hers. But he was always an easy conversationalist and excessively polite so the girls trusted him to behave himself. One night at the dance, after a slow set he was dancing with Barbara, the band broke into a fast, deafening version of "Tiger Rag." Ted let go of Barbara and broke into an eccentric dance all by himself, a combination of tap and acrobatic, with handsprings and backward somersaults, altogether quite professional. This went on for all of "Tiger Rag," which was several minutes. The others on the dance floor stopped to watch and applaud his more strenuous efforts. When it was over and the next dance started, he was back with Barbara, who appeared to have enjoyed the performance of her escort. Later, some of us asked Ted where he learned to do such acrobatic dancing and he said, "It must have been when I ran away and joined the circus." We knew that wasn't so, but he never said any more about it and he never did it again.

Once, at The Big Pavilion in Saugatuck where many of the better-known big bands would perform, I heard that Hal Kemp had picked Ted out of a crowd next to the bandstand and had asked him to step up to the microphone and sing verses to "Little White Lies." Ted did this in a clear baritone with all the professional phrasing of a Bing Crosby or a Dick Haymes. Again, it was a mystery as to how someone like Hal Kemp knew Ted DeBoer, and how Ted could be a real live song-and-dance man, owner of a Duesenberg and still a waiter at the Castle. When he didn't appear at the Castle for his third summer of work there, Carter Brown said in response to our inquiries, that Ted was manager of a hotel in Florida. We wondered if he still had the Duesenberg.

DOCTOR GOEBEL

World War One had strange effects on a few of the Castle Parkers because anti-German sentiment was so pervasive and sometimes ludicrous. Dr. Julius Goebel, the bearded, highly respected author of several books on economics, was head of the German Department at the University of Illinois in Urbana. He was one of the old-time cottage owners and the patriarch of a large family who spent their childhood summers at Castle Park. Dick Goebel, his golden-haired, handsome son, was our tennis champion at eighteen. There were other children and the family all participated in the activities of the celebratory events each year on the 4th of July and Labor Day.

In 1918, Dr. Goebel was said by some to be a German spy who sent blinker signals in the middle of the night to enemy boats on Lake Michigan from his beachfront cottage. This was later seen to be altogether goofy and hardly credible inasmuch as nobody really saw him doing it and that German naval forces would be on Lake Michigan was wildly imaginary. Yet there were those who repeated this slander of the good doctor and with all seriousness.

To his credit, Dr. Goebel did not believe there were those at Castle Park who thought he was an enemy agent. He and his family joined in the usual shared activities of the summer. In 1919, the doctor, son Dick, and daughters Eunice and "Bunt" all were competitors in the events of the "Aquatic Carnival" on August 23 that went all that day and into the evening. So, when the war was over there were no more whisperings about his treasonous behavior. In later days, it was forgotten.

THE SCHOOLHOUSE

An event in the summer of 1922 persuaded the Castle Park parents to organize what they called a "play class" to be put into effect the following summer. This involved many of the children from the ages of six to twelve who, one day in August, were all gathered together in front of the Castle under the venerable oak tree in the early afternoon. Being fundamentally bored and wondering what to do with the rest of the day they decided to hike over to Macatawa, not through the woods or on the beach as was customary, but to take the gravel road because it was a different way to get there.

Age seven, I was among them, as was my ten-year-old sister. I was only a follower, as the decision to embark on this adventure was made by some of the older girls. The younger boys followed along, having nothing better to do. Leaving the Castle grounds and going away from the lake on the road to Graafschap and Holland, the first left turn was the road to Macatawa. It paralleled the lake front about a mile to the west and about two miles distant from Black Lake, Jenison Park, and Macatawa.

We never got to Macatawa that day. We were pretty well strung out, about a dozen of us altogether, walking slowly down the road when we passed the two-room schoolhouse. It was set back about a hundred yards on the right in a vacant field on a gravel side-road. It had been built there to serve those children in the lower grades among the year-round families who comprised that local school district. We all wandered over and circled the building with nothing particular in mind until Don Wing, yielding to boyish curiosity, lifted an unlocked window and let himself into the building. He unlocked the front door and let us all inside.

This was in mid-August, when we knew the school year was soon to be upon us back at home, and perhaps we thought we might be doing the children enrolled here a favor by rendering their schoolhouse unusable for a while.

I don't know who started it, but one of the girls pulled open all the drawers in a teacher's desk and, with a nervous giggle, threw the contents far and wide on the floor. A boy then took chalk at the blackboard and went to work drawing a crude picture of a less than handsome female, labeling it "TEACHER." This became a sort of signal to the rest of us. We went through the two rooms, overturning desks and chairs and emptying shelves of books onto the floor. There was an upright piano in the second room where John Sanford, a large boy at age twelve, took its top off and ripped out all the keys inside. By then there was an atmosphere of carnival and irresponsible destruction. Anything movable was overturned. Anything fragile was broken. The overhead lights were smashed with a broom handle. The blackboard was covered with indelicate pictures of males and females.

I mostly watched and laughed with nervous excitement at what was going on. I knew that if my mother could see this, she would not believe it was happening and the thing for me to do was to get out of there. But I didn't and neither did my sister. When all the damage that could be done had been done, including breaking all the windows, we did not proceed to Macatawa. It was now about three o'clock and time to go swimming, so we forgot about going to Macatawa and went back to the Castle and home to get into our bathing suits and go to the beach.

It wasn't long before someone called the sheriff, Herman Van Noss, who lived near the Castle Park entrance and who had been a fixture there for several years. During the winter and the rest of the off-season, he was a sort of protector of the Castle Park grounds and the cottages, mostly unoccupied from October to June. He was also the Allegan County deputy sheriff in charge of this area. We never knew who told him that Castle Park kids had wrecked the schoolhouse, but he heard about it in a way that was convincing, even though he knew all our parents and doubtless wondered how such nice people could have children who thought nothing of vandalizing a schoolhouse. The next day he went to see Carter Brown, owner of the Castle and his friend of many years, and Arthur Hall, head of the Castle Park Association. The three of them drove over to the schoolhouse to see it as it had been left, totally wrecked. Sheriff Van Noss told them that among the possible consequences of this episode would be that the sheriff and the police would question every parent and child in Castle Park on suspicion of breaking and entering in order to get answers as to who exactly did what, and bring to trial in the court of Allegan all those involved.

An alternative, he said, would be if the children confessed to this malicious misdemeanor and offered to pay all the damages promptly and in time to make the necessary repairs and replacements of equipment so the school year could begin on schedule. This had the necessary effect on us guilty ones. The next day we all had to face our outraged parents and give them enough detail as to somewhat alleviate our fears of going to prison in Allegan. Not all of the Castle Park children were involved in this episode. Those who could truthfully deny any part in it looked upon us guilty ones with an attitude of relief that they hadn't been with us, combined with an inevitable feeling of moral superiority.

Mr. Hall worked out a plan which was received with some relief on the part of Sheriff Van Noss. He was still at a loss to understand why these families he had known for years could have offspring who could do such mischief, but he didn't want anybody to go to trial either. Castle Park in the early 1920s was a much more closely-knit community than now. There were no telephones except for the hand-cranked one at the Castle and radio was still in its infancy. My father and Mr. Hall put the word out that there was to be a meeting of all parents in the Castle sun parlor late the next afternoon, which was a Saturday, and that meant that most parents were at Castle Park for the weekend. At the meeting–no children allowed–an agreement was reached about two matters. One was to pay for the damage to the schoolhouse. This was the easy decision and it took the form of an assessment on the parents of the guilty ones of $100.00 per child, with a special assessment on the parents of John Sanford who had to donate a new upright piano to replace that from which their playful son had ripped out the keys.

The second agreement reached at this meeting was to start an organized daily "play class" next summer, supervised by professionals in that activity and funded by the Castle Park Association, to whom a fee would be paid for each child age six to twelve enrolled in the program. It was not compulsory for a child to be enrolled, but I knew of no child who was not because such a child would spend the summer with no one to play with. Some of us said, plaintively, that this was a terrible idea and we didn't need anybody like that to organize our play time. But of course, the answer was, "Well, look what you did to the schoolhouse." And so in early June the next summer, Mr. and Mrs. Spade appeared, probably not aware of the dimensions of their assignment which was to keep us busy with baseball, tennis, and swimming for a couple of hours in the morning and again in the afternoon, to save us from ourselves.

THE WOODS

In July and August of each summer during the 1920s, it became common for Dr. Whetzel or Dr. Jay to come to the front of the Castle lawn at about 9:30 in the morning with Carter Brown's megaphone and cry out, "Hike! Hike!" in several directions. Many of the cottages would get this message which was that if you wanted to go on a two-hour hike you should be at the Castle front lawn at ten o'clock.

There was usually a group of at least half a dozen parents, sometimes more, who would meet there and decide which way they wanted to go. The choices were (a) through the woods to the south to Macatawa, about two miles away, or (b) through the woods to the north to Baldy, a high dune reached by a somewhat difficult climb on the forest side, about a mile south of the Castle. Once at the top of Baldy, the hikers would rest and then return down the steep, sandy side to the beach, about a mile south of the Castle Park beach. The Macatawa hike was probably the most popular because it was an easy walk on a well-worn trail through the woods. Once there, the hikers could either turn around and go back to the Castle or they could briefly visit the shops in the town before returning.

The woods in this area were second-growth pines and maples with many ash and a few oaks. All of the old growth hardwood forests in the southern parts of Michigan and Wisconsin were cut away by the end of the nineteenth century, particularly after the Chicago Fire of 1871. This dreadful event required the rebuilding of most of the city and the lumber to do it with came from the nearby states to the north.

Mostly, these hikes were only incidentally for exercise. Because there were no telephones, the hikes were occasions for conversation and , usually harmless gossip. It was one of the few ways that friends could meet and talk and newcomers could become acquainted with veteran Castle Parkers. Children were not encouraged to come. Most of us didn't want to hike with our parents anyway, but these chummy interludes made it possible for a judge from Cleveland to talk to a lawyer from Chicago, or an executive of Marshall Fields to exchange comments with a retired officer of Proctor & Gamble. These conversations were seldom exclusive, or very deep and serious.

In the 1930s when telephones were beginning to be installed in most cottages, these types of informal hikes were no longer organized. However, there were more than a few cottage owners who never got a telephone. Not surprisingly, some of them had fairly large families but the parents did not feel the need for a phone, in fact, felt a need *not* to have one. We never had one at our house.

I had my very own private hangout one summer when I was about eight. It was at the south end of the beach, beyond the last beachfront house. There was a dune there called Crow's Roost, for the birds who nested in the tall pines near its top. Near its higher part was a sheltered area, sloping slightly toward the lake, covered with dense bushes. In the midst of this I found a sort of cave, formed under the shrubbery and vines, large enough for me to stretch out comfortably on the sand, hidden from everybody. The only sounds were the lapping of the waves on the beach and the buzzing of a few harmless insects. I could retreat to this private place and bring in my small knapsack a bottle of Orange Crush and a copy of one of the Tarzan or Tom Swift books and be where no one could find me. There I could ride with Tom at ninety miles an hour on his wonderful electrically-powered motorcycle or swing with Tarzan through the African tree tops to save his animal friends from hunters and poachers. Later, I would find Tarzan identified as Lord Greystoke, a member of British royalty. This was heady stuff for me.

The following summer, my arboreal cave on the beach at Crow's Roost was overgrown and no longer available to me. I had to take my Orange Crush and my books to other secluded spots down the beach for vicarious literary adventure.

1922–Ready for hike through the woods to Macatawa

GOLF

The Castle Park golf course was like no other golf course anywhere. It was laid out within the confines of the land owned by the Castle Park Association. The course was bounded on the north by two miles of woods and lakeshore owned by Swan Miller of Macatawa, on the south side by several farms and wooded areas, on the east by Kelly Lake and the road to Macatawa, and on the west by Lake Michigan.

Almost everybody played golf at Castle Park but it was different kind of golf. There was a nine-hole course laid out with several holes on the campus area near the Castle and other holes on long fairways in a vacant area between two rows of cottages to the north of the Castle. The fairways were occasionally mowed by a mower drawn by two horses, but not more than once or twice each summer. Mostly, the grass on the sandy fairways was left to grow as nature intended. It could be described as a "par three" course because a few of the better golfers could indeed play the nine holes with a score in the low thirties and only a few of the holes were long enough to be par fours. My father and his friends would make regular scores in the low 40s. The clubs he carried in a small canvas bag had wood shafts and all had names. The woods were called the "driver" and the "brassie." The irons were called the "putter", the "mid-iron," the "mashie," the "mashie-niblick," the "niblick," and the "spoon."

The greens were not real greens. They were smooth and clay-covered with a thin layer of sand and were the main challenge of the game on the golf course. The tees were on flat shallow boxes filled with smooth, hard clay, and beside each one was a large double-box on legs with a towel hanging on it and a device for washing the balls.

No one took golf lessons because there was no one to give them. There were no tee-times. If on a weekend the course was crowded in the morning, you just waited until the afternoon when everyone was at the beach and you could tee off any time you wanted.

When I was about eight-years-old, I could caddy for my father and be paid twenty-five cents for the nine holes. I began to play golf when I was ten, but never quite understood the game and had no real aptitude for it. Mostly I played tennis, beginning when I was eight. I found this to be something I could do with some success.

Serious golfers coming to the Castle and seeing the course for the first time didn't quite know what to make of it. They could not consider it to be any kind of challenge but a sort of recreational game for women and children. However, some few played it as seriously as they could and tried to equal the unofficial course record that had been set by a Chicago golfer guest of Mr. Hall in the summer of 1925. Mr. Hall lived near the second tee, played every weekend running, and was himself a devotee of the game. He would play the nine holes with score in the middle 30s.

For several years in the 1920s, one of the guests at the Castle during the month of August was Miss Gould, a wealthy old lady from Lake Forest and an enthusiastic golfer on the Castle Park course every morning. One day when I was eight and caddying for my mother, she joined Miss Gould and they played together. We reached the third tee on top of a small hill with the hole below it and about a hundred yards out. I thought I was standing in a safe place at the tee but I had forgotten, or hadn't noticed, that Miss Gould was left-handed. She swung her mid-iron back to hit her ball off the tee but instead hit me on the right side of my forehead on her backswing with enough force to knock me down and produce a large gash near my right temple.

I was hurt and angry, and cried vigorously. Miss Gould was shocked and embarrassed, and my mother comforted her more than she did me. I was taken to a hospital in Holland after my mother had bandaged my head and stopped the bleeding. The doctor there laid me out and washed the wound and said, "This is going to sting a little," as he applied some disinfectant, which was probably iodine and sewed up the gash with several stitches. That indeed made me erupt with loud and tearful complaints. He finally turned me loose with a large bandage on my head so I was the center of attention when I went to the beach where everybody was after lunch.

My explanation for my injury was that I fell and hurt myself, to which I added proudly that it took four stitches to fix it. My mother had told me not to mention Miss Gould and I did not because I knew she was a fine old lady and that what happened to me was really due to my own carelessness.

The attraction of the golf course grew as those who played it frequently began to consider Castle Park golf a game that no one took seriously. It was considered either a form of mild outdoor exercise with one's friends or even a game to be played alone in this intimate community with no one to see your hooks and slices and no one to see you try to putt with any accuracy on a clay green. One of my early triumphs when I was twelve was to play the eighth hole, about 200 yards, in three strokes—one drive, one approach and one putt—with my mother as a witness. I was never that lucky again in any game of golf anywhere

Later in college, I thought I should make one last effort to achieve respectable competence in this game and bought a set of Spalding woods and irons and a large, heavy bag and began to take lessons. I read instruction books and played the game in earnest. There were many golf courses in the Chicago area, some quite famous as that at Olympia Fields, some quite exclusive as those at Glenview and the South Shore Club. Many more were open to the public and worthy of one's best efforts. I played several of the public courses over a period of several years and was able to break 100 only once. When I was called into the Navy in 1941, I put my clubs away in the attic at home and they have been in various other attics ever since.

1928–Betsy Needham: Golf at Castle Park

THE NAKED NAVY

When we were ten years old, my friends and I used to walk up the beach to Halfway Creek, leaving the Castle diving stands behind us and continue the six miles to the creek, which was the half-way point to Saugatuck. It wasn't much of a creek and it changed its course through the sandy beach to the lake during every heavy rain. It came from the woods about fifty yards from the beach and sometimes we would follow its course up through the trees into the environs of Camp Halcyon ("For Girls").

The height of devilment was to take off our clothes and go stealthily and stark naked up the creek waters, which were never more than a few inches deep, until we could see signs of life at the girls' camp. Not once did we show ourselves. It was more fun to talk about it later, an activity which was to present itself to me throughout life.

Membership in the Naked Navy was not given to me right away. My mother was the last holdout in the Castle Park community who made me take a nap after lunch when I was nine years old. The other boys were at the beach or playing tennis while I was wide awake in my hot bedroom. At two o'clock I could go out, but the group was already out to Halfway Creek to take off their clothes and go swimming, or wandering through the woods to Macatawa to Jesiek's Boatyard to look enviously at the speedboats docked there, and to listen to the Jesiek boys telling dirty jokes. It was not until I was ten that I could finish lunch and be on my way with no questions asked.

One day early in June, the summer that I was ten, I met the boys in front of the Castle and we started off toward the beach. The prospect of going swimming naked was wholly unexpected. We walked the six miles to Halfway Creek and the other boys took off their clothes and dashed into the water. Finally, I did the same, and when I was in the water, two of the others took my clothes and threw them into the creek. They then tied my shirt and pants into hard knots. This was my initiation into the Naked Navy.

I was also sworn to secrecy. One did not tell anyone, especially not one's mother, about this. During those years I was the one who was the last to find out about the mysterious pastimes of the more free and adventuresome of the boys. I thought the mothers had an agreement about after lunch naps and that everybody took them. I later learned that some did and some did not. Permissive mothers did not necessarily have trouble-making boys. Restrictive mothers, more often than not, were the mothers of the trouble-makers, and while I was not much of a trouble maker at the age of ten, I was by the age of thirteen.

IGNOMINY AT GOSHORN LAKE

Mr. and Mrs. Spade appeared in June the summer after the infamous raid on the schoolhouse. He was a World War One veteran and told us of some of his experiences in France. He was a dark and handsome fellow in his thirties with a black toothbrush mustache. He was to look after the boys, and his wife, the girls. She was a round-faced happy young woman who wore her long hair in a bun behind her head. She had brought a little ukulele with her and spent hours with her little girl charges picking away at the strings and singing the popular songs of the 20s. We called them Mr. Spade and Mrs. Spade, never anything more familiar.

He taught us the finer points of baseball, played at that time with medium-sized softballs with fast pitching and no gloves. We developed a series of games for the boys in competition with Macatawa and Ottowa Beach. The girls would sometimes play Camp Halcyon. Pitching for the boys team became a highly-coveted honor among us. I never pitched and considered myself lucky to be the first baseman for the first few summers. Later, when we got to be teenagers and with two successors to Mr. Spade, there developed a sort of social pecking-order on the baseball team with the most aggressive boys in the infield and the quiet ones playing outfield.

By that time, I was playing right field and hoping no balls would come my way. It happened that Mr. Chappel, the third summer after he came to succeed Mr. Spade, had an experience with me in June that led to my banishment to right field shortly thereafter.

The incident with Mr. Chappel happened on an overnight camping trip, for the boys only, to Goshorn Lake, about five miles north of Saugatuck. The ancient Ford Model T stake bed truck took us to Goshorn with all our gear. We were to camp out by this little lake and hike back to the Castle along the Lake Michigan shore, which was about two miles to the west.

We arrived in mid-afternoon and spent the rest of the day exploring the adjoining woods and swimming in the lake. There was an abandoned barn nearby and two of the boys had already been to explore it. They came back to the lake and told me there was a gallon jug of hard cider under some hay in the barn, and didn't I want to come and look at it? We did and sure enough, it was hard cherry cider that was beginning to bubble. The three of us were sharing the same tent so I took the hard cider and hid it under my blanket in the tent.

By sundown, we were ready to eat. One of the cooks from the Castle had built a fire and was fixing hamburgers for everybody. I had sampled the cider in secret, when no one was in the tent, drinking perhaps a pint out of the gallon jug. It made my stomach burn pleasantly and a short while later, my ears began to ring and I was a little dizzy. I could eat no supper and didn't join the group when the hamburgers were ready. When they came looking for me, I was in the tent, sitting on the floor with the jug of cider between my knees and brandishing my hunting knife. Without knowing it, I had become as drunk as a sailor in the harbor after a two-year voyage.

Mr. Chappel came and tried to take the jug away and I told him he better not try. He really didn't want to tangle with an intoxicated thirteen-year-old with a large knife. Everybody left me alone and for a while I could hear them talking about me. Then I went to sleep. The next morning I felt fine, but very hungry.

After breakfast, as everyone was getting ready for the hike back to the Castle along the Lake Michigan shore, Mr. Chappel said to me, "Hair, you go back to the truck." He turned away and that was that. The cook from the castle was sitting in the truck waiting for me. I got in and we drove back. I knew what was up. In his way, Mr. Chappel was letting me know that nobody behaves the way I did on any of his overnight camping trips and gets away with it. I had to tell my parents that I was sick and couldn't make the hike back with the rest of the boys. They accepted that, and no more was said about it until the next day. At ten in the morning, I went down to the baseball diamond and found Mr. Chappel in an earnest discussion with my father.

My father was seldom a harsh man, but he was coldly angry when he turned away from Mr. Chappel and said to me, "Sam, go up to the cottage right now and stay there."

I knew then that Mr. Chappel had given him a run-down on my disgraceful behavior and I learned never to trust him again. When my father got up to the cottage, he was inarticulate and shaking with rage. He said, "Come with me!"

We left by the back porch door and walked out into the woods. I didn't know what he was going to do. We walked to South Hill, about two hundred yards behind the cottage, and my father sat on the slope with his head in his hands.

"How could you do it?" He asked, looking away from me as if I had robbed a gas station and murdered the attendant. I said that I didn't mean anything by it, that now I knew it was wrong and that I was sorry about the whole thing. I also told him I felt fine the morning after my solitary drinking bout, and could have hiked home with everybody else.

That didn't convince him of anything. My father was a deeply religious man and had never had a drink in his life. He wouldn't have liquor in the house. He was silent for a few minutes, sitting on the hillside. Finally he said, "You've disgraced us." His fear was that he wouldn't be able to explain this to his friends.

He was a pioneer Castle Parker and had been coming over by boat, car, or train from Chicago since 1905. He was a director of the Castle Park Association, which owned the golf course, the water works and other common acreage purchased by the Association from the Parr family years before. Later, during the Depression years, the Castle operation as a hotel was losing money. My father and Mr. Luther Barber from Winnetka went on a note for Carter Brown, the owner of the hotel, at the bank in Allegan. As Carter was to tell me many years later, he "just sort of lived on the deficit."

I had humiliated my father, and he didn't know what to do about it. I was too big for a spanking and too young to understand how deeply I had hurt him by not having sense enough to stay away from hard cherry cider. If only one of the other boys had joined me in partaking of that evil product stolen out of a barn, it would have been all right, a "boys will be boys" situation. But I was all alone in this fall from rectitude.

My father said nothing more, and we walked back to the cottage. I never heard from him about it again, but he knew that I knew I had hurt him. He liked me too much to do anything more about it. And I had not caused him any real trouble before. Fortunately, time cures a lot of things, and before the summer was over, the whole episode was put aside as one of Sam's aberrations. But Mr. Chappel forever after only spoke to me when he had to, once to tell me to play right field, not first base.

MORE ABOUT THE CASTLE PARK WAITERS

Late one morning, I was on my way to the beach beyond the Castle near the baseball diamond when I came upon Jack Stibbs, an older boy, and Lane Brearton, a waiter, facing each other and having a fierce argument. Jack pushed Lane, Lane took a swing at Jack, and they went at it, wrestling each other to the ground, pounding and kicking each other. Mr. Jordan was playing golf and was halfway to the first hole when he saw them and ran over, brandishing his mashie.

"Stop that!" he roared, and grabbed Jack by the shoulders, pulling him away. Jack was trembling with rage. He glared at Lane, tried to step toward him, and shouted, "I'll beat your ass off!"

Mr. Jordan said, "That's enough, Jack!" then to Lane, "Lane, you better get out of here!" He took Jack by the arm and started him toward the Stibbs cottage on the lakefront. "Go on home!" he said. He waited until the boys had gone their separate ways.

Mr. Jordan was a tough old grocery wholesaler, a founding member of the Castle Park Association, one of the elders of the Castle Park community, and the respected umpire of all the baseball games. So Jack went off muttering something about how he was going to kill Lane Brearton. I never knew what the argument was about, but I suspect it was about Jack's younger sister Betty, whom Lane had been escorting to the movies at Saugatuck, and Jack did not approve of that. The barriers between the young men who were the waiters and the young men of the families of the cottage-owners were high and impenetrable. The waiters almost never played golf or tennis. It was assumed that they were not supposed to have time to do this. However, they did play baseball Saturday afternoons, seriously and well. There was a weekend game that had been going on for many years between the married men and the single men, the latter including several waiters. Saturday afternoons at two o'clock, the teams would take the field and play a hard pitch softball game. The married men had some strong young players, but so did the waiters, who usually won. The games were played in great good spirits, with loud cheers from the gallery, and equally loud ongoing chatter among the players.

These games gave the waiters an outlet for their athletic abilities and an opportunity to participate in a sports event on an equal basis. Most of them were from good families and were in college in the South, but they were still Carter Brown's employees and lived behind the Castle in "The Shack," a sort of dormitory of Spartan simplicity. Each man had a little cubicle big enough for a bunk bed, a chest of drawers and a chair. There were no closets and no plumbing except for a washroom at one end with a commode, a couple of washbowls and a shower for the six waiters, It was much like camping out.

One of the waiters we called "Fast Forty Angel Face." One summer afternoon in August, 1923, he swam from the diving stand at Castle Park to the pier at Macatawa, two miles in forty minutes. Forever after, he was "Fast Forty," with great admiration from us kids. I was then eight years old and his achievement was one which we thought we might live to emulate if we practiced our swimming enough, for no one had ever swum that far that fast. He had acquired the "Angel Face" nickname when he was a high school student in Atlanta and looked much younger than his teenage years. Even at age twenty at Castle Park, he looked like a fresh face boy. He did well as a steady and polite waiter, and practiced his distance swimming nearly every afternoon. On the day he swam to Macatawa, he had a friend on the beach at Castle Park and another on the pier at Macatawa to confirm his elapsed time for the two-mile swim. He did not like to be called Angel Face. One day late in the afternoon in the lobby of the Castle, I overheard him talking to a couple of his friends. He was almost in tears, and said with great sadness, "Why do they call me Angel Face?" His friends cheered him up and told him to forget it. Everybody liked him, they said, which was true. When at work in the dining room he was called by his real name which was Robert. I never heard him mention it again. We thought he was a shy fellow and a hell of a swimmer, so we admired him from a distance and called him Fast Forty.

There were other waiters, several from Georgia Tech, who frequently worked for Carter Brown for the four summers that they were in college. One was Frank Whitley, a small, serious baseball player and a real jock. He talked about football almost all the time so that whenever he attempted a date with one of the Castle Park daughters, she was invariably busy and never took him seriously.

It was said that Mrs. Sheridan, from a long-time cottage-owning family, had a thing going with Whitley Morris. He spent a lot of time weekday evenings on the front porch of her cottage concealed behind some pine trees, but this was only when Mr. Sheridan was in Chicago. Whit was a heavy-set, easy-going, schmoozing Southerner with lots of practiced charm.

Another waiter had a name hard to believe, Saplin Morecock. Behind his back, we called him Maplin Sorecock. He was of a good family in Atlanta, his father a prosperous surgeon. He complained a lot, but was engaging and funny. He was probably socially superior to most of the other Southern boys, but never showed it.

There were also two brothers from Kansas, Hugh and Johnny Marshall. Hugh was a stocky, scholarly-looking fellow with horn-rimmed glasses. He was hard working, enjoyed the job, was proud to be a waiter, and was a very good one. He was called "Hoots" and my mother often asked for him when we went to Castle's dining room for dinner. Johnny was Hugh's younger brother, taller and more skeptical of the whole enterprise, but a quick-thinker and competent waiter whom everyone liked. Neither of the brothers attempted any relationship with the Castle Park girls. They understood the barrier and never tried to go beyond it.

1931–Waiters: Whitley Morris, Lane Brearton, Jimmy Waring, "Fast Forty," Frank Whitley, Hugh Marshall, Saplin Morecock

THE STABLE

Driving past the Castle parking area and the waiters' dormitory to the foot of South Hill was a large open area of a couple of acres where the truck garage, the stable, and the ice-house were. Usually, Carter Brown brought six saddle horses to Castle Park in early June from his stable at the Pine Crest Inn in Tryon, North Carolina. They would come, two at a time, in horse trailers. Each would be put into a stall and all the necessary saddlery was kept in front. There were handlers who took care of them all summer, black grooms who had been with Carter for a long time and who made the horses available for riding on the various trails in the wooded areas surrounding Castle Park for several miles in all directions. There was also a pony named Marietta for younger riders. Some of the horses were hunters to be ridden by more experienced riders. Others were older more gentle saddle horses anybody could ride. Sometimes Carter Brown would put together a group of three or four riders and they would go out with him for a couple of hours in the morning or afternoon. He was very proud of his horses and in Tryon, where they came from, they were known to be a part of his highly respected stable in an area inhabited by horse lovers who supported several other riding stables, as well as owners who had their own horses and facilities.

Castle Park children, including my sister and me, were attracted to the stable, just to come down in the morning and look at the horses, wander around the open garage shelter for the Castle vehicles and the ice-house above the stable, and occasionally to venture out on a horseback ride. When this was done, one of the grooms would come with us and, very tactfully, give us an elementary riding lesson. He would tell us how to hold and use the reins, how to keep our knees tight against the saddle and how to post when the horse was trotting. We were never highly experienced riders and never wore the proper riding clothes. Other older teenage girls who were more seriously involved in horsemanship had their own tack and were learning the fine points of hunting and jumping. They wore the hard derby hats, the jodhpurs and riding clothes from Abercrombie & Fitch or from Von Lengerke & Antoine and their fathers had put them on horseback when they were pre-teens. Castle Park boys, on the other hand, did not display any interest in flat saddles and the other accoutrements of orthodox equestrianism. We fancied ourselves to be potential cowboys on pinto ponies, riding stock saddles and carrying trusty Winchesters. No hard hats and no jodhpurs, just Stetsons and cowboy boots for us! Since Carter

Brown had no western saddles—would rather die than have one—we had to wait to be cowboys and were only spectators at the horse shows.

In August, Carter would set up an arena on the first fairway of golf course near the front of the Castle, with a temporary fence around it with jumps and hazards for the hunters who would compete there. Additional participants came from Waukazoo, Ottowa Beach, and Grand Rapids and judges came over from Chicago. This was The Castle Park Horse Show, one of the big events prior to Labor Day. After a few years in the 20s, it became more of an event than could be easily handled and by 1930, the horse show was abandoned as too much of an effort by all involved because it interfered with the use of the first hole of the golf course for several days. It was also abandoned because of some of the old-time members of the Castle Park Association and cottage owners could not get used to seeing any strangers anywhere on the grounds, even for a two-day horse show.

The real attraction of the stable came about during the summer when I was twelve and on my way home to our cottage on South Hill after dark on a quiet evening. I happened to hear some excited voices down in the stable area. Slowly and carefully, I made my way there, trying not to be seen. What I found was a vigorous crap game going on with a half-dozen of the black employees of the Castle in a semi-circle on a large blanket in the front of the stable. Illuminated by a Coleman gas lantern, they were throwing dice against the stable wall with all the common accompanying entreaties encouraging the dice to come up with the right numbers. When I edged in closer and could be seen within the light of the lantern, the players didn't seem to mind that I was watching them. They all knew me as a kid who hung around the stable anyway. One of them, Orrin, looked over at me and said, "Come on in, Mister Sam." I did not reply, but moved gingerly closer, and then said, "I just want to watch." All I knew was that seven and eleven were winning numbers, but I had to watch for a while to figure out the rest of the crap game ritual. Three of the players were grooms who worked only with the horses and the stable. We knew them as Hawk, Orrin, and Rudy. Orrin motioned me into the game and when the dice came around to him, he handed them to me and said, "Here. You do it." I put down a quarter on the blanket, lost it with a seven after a few attempts to make a five, and the dice went on to the next player. Orrin said, "Mister Sam, you gotta talk to them dice before you throw them, and when you throw them you gotta say "HAH!" real loud. If you don't say nothing, they ain't gonna be you friend!"

I soon learned about "Eighter from Decatur," "Snake Eyes" and all the other descriptive demands made on the dice to make a point. When I heard "Colt 45!" it was to make a nine. When I heard, "What do you get fer stealin' chickens, dice?" I learned that was to make a ten—the number of days usually served for such a conviction.

I was on an allowance of fifty cents a week, so my resources for getting into a serious dice game were somewhat limited, but I had delivered several telegrams in the past few weeks so I had a couple of dollars in change in my bedroom bureau drawer. The stable game was usually every Friday, payday for the Castle employees. So the following Friday, and for the remaining two Fridays until Labor Day, I made it secretively and stealthily down to the stable at about eight o'clock to get into the game. After that, the horses were sent back to Tryon, the stable was unoccupied, and Orrin, Rudy, and Hawk were gone, so my gambling experience came to a sudden end. But I had within my boyhood experience at least a beginning of familiarity with a game enjoyed by older acquaintances who let me be one of them for a few weeks when I was twelve-years-old. I probably lost three dollars over a period of three weeks, but at least I was ahead of most of my companions in this kind of experience.

The excitement of the game at the stable was entirely due to my realization that this was not just a forbidden activity, but one which was far beyond the remote comprehension of my parents who, if I said I had been in "a crap game," would have no idea of what I was talking about. But if they knew it was a form of gambling and their pre-teen son was participating, I would be beyond redemption. My father would not know how to deal with this sinful behavior. Even though he thought he knew all about sin and how we are all sinners, he knew nothing about gambling except that it was something decent people didn't do. I told Don Wing about this and he said he knew about the game at the stable, but had not taken any part in it because he was not one to put his allowance money at risk. The following summers, the dice game at the stable didn't happen again, or if it did, I didn't know about it. I was also a little older and the fascination of doing something forbidden was now somewhat less compelling.

Seventeen years later, while stationed on the Galapagos Islands as a Navy pilot in a squadron doing "negative patrol" in four-engine seaplanes to protect the Panama canal, there was a crap game going on a pool table in the Quonset hut that served as a recreation hall. Ten-dollar bills were the usual currency used in this nightly game.

This, and endless poker games, were about the only recreation available for the year-and a-half we were there, but I found that I could hold my own in this game based upon my evenings in the stable at Castle Park with some stable-boys who, in their way, were experts. When the squadron was decommissioned and the fifty of us stationed on "The Rock" were reassigned to stateside duty, I emerged with about seven hundred dollars, winnings I attribute to my earlier training in this ancient game. And also, if the situation ever arises where I am encouraged or compelled to get into another crap game, I will go into it with confidence and joy.

MY FIRST CAR

For two summers, in 1929 and 1930, I was away from Castle Park for the most part and we only were there at the beginning and end of those seasons. We all went to Europe in 1929 on the Canadian Pacific liner Montcalm, a small, comfortable one-class ship, sailing from Montreal to Cherbourg and Southampton. The summer of 1930, I went with a close friend and classmate Woody McCulloh, to spend most of the summer at Klondike Ranch near Buffalo, Wyoming. I was then fifteen.

In the summer of 1931, I had recently obtained my driver's license and was ready to do all the things a teenage boy feels compelled to do with a car. My father took me to a used car lot on the west side of Chicago and we talked to a J. Valentine Walkowsky, a name which intrigued me then and has remained in my memory. He showed us several older and somewhat beat-up cars, as my father said we just wanted "something for the boy to drive this summer." We finally bought a 1927 Chevrolet four-door touring car with a soft top. It was black, as were most cars in those days, with a four-cylinder engine, about as simple and fundamental a piece of automotive equipment as was ever manufactured, and it cost $35.00 cash. This was 1931 and the Great Depression, while not at its depth, was taking hold in many ways. Thirty-five dollars would buy a lot.

I happily drove this car off the lot and home where I began to examine its insides and venture into the realm of the incipient, extremely careful, and ready-to-learn shade-tree mechanic. Soon I learned all about that car that could be learned without taking it apart and doing an engine job on it. Shortly thereafter, in early June, we were all off to Castle Park to stay until mid-September. I drove alone in "my car" to Castle Park, 150 miles, without episode. It would not go very fast, but sounded healthy as it ran and I never demanded more of it than it could deliver. I was very careful to shift down going up a hill and to push in the clutch sometimes going down a shallow grade in order to save gas.

On arrival at the Castle I immediately and with great pride showed the car to Don Wing, a friend who was considered by everyone who knew him to be the local automotive fix-up genius. He had an old Indian motorcycle that he totally took apart and put back together again so that it ran with much more authority and made all the noise appropriate for a big old World War I vintage motorcycle. He also took great pride and pleasure in repairing and tuning the various Castle Park hotel vehicles, including a flatbed Model T Ford truck cranked by hand, a Ford "woody" station wagon, and a Dodge panel truck. We drove my car one warm afternoon to Gilligan Lake, about six miles away, on unpaved, seldom-used, one-lane dirt roads and through deep sand in some places. But we got there and back and Don pronounced his judgment that my car had "good valves" and should run for a while without any major attention. It did have a self starter, a button on the floor of the driver's seat that you had to step on firmly. It was directly above the battery that was under a removable piece of the wood floor. Sometimes when I stepped on the starter button, nothing would happen. I would then remove the wood cover over the battery and bang on the battery connections with a wood hammer I had for that purpose and clean the cable connections with a mixture of water and baking soda. Then the starter would work.

In previous summers, Don Wing had already taught me how to drive the Model T Ford flatbed truck, that was cranked by hand. This was a learning experience that involved one of us sitting at the steering wheel and moving the spark and accelerator levers at the right time for the person doing the cranking so the engine would come alive. The Model T was the culmination of the genius of Henry Ford. Anyone could, with a few minutes of concentrated instruction, learn to drive this very practical car. There were three foot pedals, from left to right: the brake, the reverse, and the clutch. The accelerator was a lever under the steering wheel worked with the right hand. To get it going, I knew how to set the spark (another lever under the steering wheel), set the accelerator at a fast idle, turn on the magneto switch and, in colder weather, have a friend in the driver's seat pull out the choke and adjust it when the engine started. Usually, after a few firm cranks to turn the engine over, it would suddenly start and the whole car would shake and be ready to go. You had to drive with your feet working the clutch and your right hand doing the acceleration. The transmission, I was told in later years, was an early simplified planetary version of what became the automatic transmission in Detroit's later cars. I did not know then and do not now understand how it worked as I was never one to pursue automotive knowledge beyond the elementary fundamentals. I knew about the way internal combustion drove the cylinders and a little about how power went from the engine to the rear wheels. And I have learned that frequent changes of cylinder oil will lengthen the life of an engine. That's all I know about cars today and, like some men who tinkered with cars in boyhood, in later life I have not felt compelled to know much more.

Early in the summer, Mary Belden came to Castle Park with her parents and her inseparable companion, a small, short-haired black and white terrier dog named Billy. Her father had just given her a Buick roadster with a soft top and a rumble seat, the epitome of what every teenage girl could possibly want.

We had grown up together for the last ten years at Castle Park, so she showed me her new car with great pride. When I asked her if I could drive it, she agreed unhesitatingly. She said, "Don't let anybody else drive it, and bring it back in half an hour, Sam." She did not know much about cars and now that I had my own car, even an old, beat-up, low grade Chevy, she wanted me to pass favorable judgment on her wonderful new automobile. There were others standing around admiring her new car and three of them, Jimmy Waring and two girls, got into Mary's car with me at the wheel with the top down. I was enthralled. The car had a huge V-8 engine and made an appropriately powerful noise when fully revved-up. I was not only enthralled, I absolutely had to see how fast this car would go. We got on M-11, the one-lane asphalt road to Saugatuck, about fourteen miles away. The road was never in good repair with pot holes and thin places in the pavement. I went faster until, at eighty-five miles per hour, Jimmy Waring in the rumble seat shouted in a terror-stricken voice, "Hey, don't drive so damn fast, Sam!" I paid no attention and so we drove at that speed over the uneven bumpy asphalt road to Saugatuck and back.

The engine of this new car had now been thoroughly broken in. When we got back, my passengers climbed out with some relief at being unscathed. Mary later told me that when she took the car back to the Buick dealer in Chicago about a week later for a routine inspection, the service department had to keep the car for several days, retune the engine and adjust the timing and the cooling systems. When Mary asked them why, the service man said, "Lady, you been driving this car too fast. Don't do it again until you have driven 500 miles at not over fifty miles an hour."

Mary was very forgiving with me. She spoke of this as an inevitability in letting me test her car. She never mentioned it to me again, but wouldn't let me drive it either. Her friends who had ridden with me told her how fast her car would go.

LATE BLOOMING–I BEGIN TO FIND OUT ABOUT GIRLS

The summer that I had my car was eventful for several reasons. The girls at Castle Park, who had ignored me for years, now took an interest in riding in my "cute car." Girls in their teens are much more grown up than boys the same age. They are quick to see how to handle situations with boys and often take pleasure in letting boys make fools of themselves. But, when I parked my car behind the Castle Hotel, I would often pick up two or three girls on their way to the beach and sometimes they would ask me to "go for a little ride, Sam." This was an open car with fabric top that I had folded down where it was stored behind the back seat as were all "touring cars" in those days. I would leave the Castle grounds and drive east over to Graafschap, about five miles away, maybe stop at the store there and get bottles of pop, or maybe just turn around and go back to the beach. The girls found this to be a brief diversion and laughed and giggled all the way. I was mostly silent, just driving.

At sixteen, I was continually being reminded that there were girls in many of the places where I happened to be. Somehow, they seemed more confident about life, were much more self possessed, and were frequently to be found in pairs. I found that at Castle Park the sixteen-and-up girls were sought after vigorously by the waiters at the hotel, but the girls were seldom seen after dark with any of them. The barrier was there "Don't fool around with the waiters. They are not people like us.", even though they were mostly college boys from decent families. Occasionally, some of the older college age girls would go to a movie in Holland or Saugatuck with a waiter, but when the show was over, back they came to sit in front to the Castle on the long bench by the front door, listening to the katydids and the whippoorwills and to smoke cigarettes and talk. No more than that.

I found that the younger girls who had never paid attention to me before were at least a little impressed by my cute car. Finally, fearful of rejection, I asked one of the more beautiful and sought-after sixteen-year-olds, Marian, if she would meet me after dinner at the Castle to go for a ride in my car. She looked to be about twenty and was brought up to be soft-spoken, ladylike, and probably not conscious that she had a face and figure that were the envy of all her friends. I had played in a pick-up baseball game with her that afternoon. I asked her if she would like to ride to Gilligan Lake in my "new car."

To my consternation, she said very demurely, "Yes, Sam. What time?"

"I'll meet you in front of the Castle after dinner."

Our families had dinner there most nights, had known each other for years, and a meeting at the Castle was socially acceptable for teenagers. They knew there would be no drinking because nobody drank and cigarette smoking was something you didn't do until you went away to college. So a young lady going for an evening ride in Sam Hair's car was perceived without any misgivings by the young lady's parents. When I met Marian at the Castle, she wore a white linen dress with a navy collar, shoes, and stockings, and looked as if she should be going to a tea-dance at the Palm Court of the Plaza instead of a ride in a beat-up open car to Gilligan Lake.

We got there after going over many country lanes and bumpy dirt roads, some of which were rarely traveled except by tractors and other farm vehicles. Gilligan Lake was not much of a lake and was at that time totally undeveloped with no nearby houses or other signs of life. There was a small pier where a few rowboats were fastened. The only thing this lake was good for was for fishing for perch. The water was clear and clean, but the bottom was squishy mud and we never swam in it. Marian and I got out of my car and sat on the pier for a while, not saying much. She moved to the end of the pier, took off her shoes and stockings and dabbled her feet in the water. I sat beside her, but did not take off my shoes. She said she was going to Miss Madeira's in September, and where was I going? I said I guessed I was going back to U-High again, the high-school part of the University of Chicago.

It was night by now, and she asked me if I could find my way back in the dark. "Do you want to go back?" I asked. She seemed to be more in charge of this event than I was.

"Yes, I think we'd better," but it was not as if she were concerned about anything. The stars were out now and we talked about some of the familiar constellations that she could point out. I had never been interested enough to find out about the stars, so she eagerly pointed out the Big Dipper, Orion's Belt, and the Pleiades.

We returned and I parked behind the Castle in a row of cars in an open shelter. There was nobody near and it was totally quiet. I turned off the ignition and edged closer to Marian. She didn't move away so I put my arm around her shoulders and pulled her closer. She stared straight ahead and said nothing. I felt that I had to say something. "I hope you enjoyed the ride."

"Yes, thanks. The last time we were at Gilligan was last summer, so I'm really glad to see it again."

I said, softly and looking straight ahead, "I was going to try to kiss you, but now I'm afraid to."

She sat still for a few moments, then turned toward me, put her hands on each side of my head, put her face to mine, and gave me a long, lingering, wet, tongue-in-my-mouth kiss. When she was done, she whispered in my ear, "Don't tell, Sam." Then she turned away, put her hands in her lap, straightened her dress, and said, "Thank you for the ride. Now you can walk me home."

The demure, shy product of the finishing school was now becoming managerial. I said not a word because I was dizzy and in shock. I was absolutely sure she knew I was scared out of my mind, and she tried the only way she could to make my evening a success. We got out of the car and walked across the first fairway of the golf course to her cottage. At the door, I still said nothing for a moment, then I managed a "Good night, Marian." She smiled and gave me a pat on my shoulder, opened the front door and went in.

I walked back to our house on South Hill in a trance. Compared to today's mid-teenagers, I was innocent, ignorant, knew little about tobacco, alcohol and girls. No, I wouldn't tell anybody. Wild horses would never get me to tell anybody anything about my date with Marian Dunn, Castle Park's sixteen-year-old goddess, who knew me better than I knew myself.

> Oh, Marion Dunn, Miss Marion Dunn,
> I'm enamored of you in the Castle Park sun.
> And while we were playing the ball game today
> How could I resist the temptation to say,
> "Come with me tonight, and we'll go for a ride,
> Let me be alone with you by my side."
> So, when you said, "Yes," I was weakened with joy,
> For you can play baseball just like a boy,
> And yet you are carelessly lovely and bright,
> And maybe you'll like me a little tonight.

HIGHER EDUCATION BY EDGAR RICE BURROUGHS

Edgar Rice Burroughs was busy in the 1920s producing the Tarzan and the Mars books. One of those seemed to be published every year and as soon as we could, we got them for birthdays or for Christmas. I read *Tarzan of the Apes* when I was seven, and I remember my exhilaration on reading D'Arnot's Message, "Congratulations. You are Greystoke." Tarzan became the most famous fictional character in the world, except for Sherlock Holmes, also an Englishman.

Then there were the Mars books, with their six-legged horses and, in *The Chessmen of Mars*, the special group of ruling inhabitants who could remove their heads at any time and reinstall them on any of a selection of available headless bodies. I could never quite figure out how John Carter, the American sword-wielding adventurer and the hero of these stories, got to Mars as Edgar Rice Burroughs never quite told us, except that it was interplanetary travel made possible by intense concentration and help from friends on Mars. Carter would lose consciousness and wake up on Mars, ready to right a number of wrongs done, or about to be done, to Dejah Thoris with whom he carried on a spirited but sanitary love affair. He would travel all over Barsoom, engage many enemies, defend Princess Thuvia from would-be kidnappers, and restore his friends, the rightful rulers of Barsoom, to their sovereignty over the planet.

I read all of these books in our cottage at Castle Park on hot summer nights by the light of a large kerosene lamp with all the windows open and with most of the moths on South Hill fluttering outside the screens. It was my main entertainment because there was no network radio and television was not even imagined. So we read a lot of books and some evenings my mother read aloud to us from old bound volumes of *St. Nicholas* magazine such stories as *Sarah Crewe* or *What Happened At Miss Minchen's* and *Little Lord Fauntleroy*, both by Frances Hodgson Burnett and serialized in that magazine.

In recent years, pictures have been released allegedly taken of the Martian landscape by satellites circumnavigating Mars or by an unmanned machine on wheels crawling over the Martian countryside taking photos and sending them back to us. As a result of my indoctrination by Edgar Rice Burroughs about what was happening on Mars, I prefer to believe that what we are really seeing are not pictures of Mars at all, but probably of a desert in Arizona and that John Carter is still up there on the Red Planet, doing the right thing. I need better evidence to be convinced that Barsoom is no more than an article of faith like Atlantis or Erehwon.

A TRIP TO CANADA WITH DON JERREMS

There came a time in mid-summer when I grew bored with the way things were going and I though it was time to take a trip in my car. My mechanic friend Don Wing had no interest in coming with me. Don Jerrems was much more adventurous and was willing to do anything. For two generations his family had been the owners of the leading men's clothing store with off-the-rack and tailor-made upscale suits on Michigan Avenue in Chicago. Don was staying at Castle Park in a cottage rented for the summer, but sometimes he would be left alone when his parents had to be in Chicago. We talked about going to "The Soo," or The Sault St. Marie at the north end of the Michigan Upper Peninsula. To my surprise, my parents had no serious objection, so we got ourselves ready. We were both sixteen with recently acquired drivers' licenses. I would do most of the driving because I knew more about the car. We were each given $50.00 to cover all our expenses and we thought we would be gone about a week. I can't envision two well brought up boys in a jalopy going off by themselves on a trip like that today, but back then it was not uncommon. We would stay in tourist camps for $2.00 per night. We would eat in any kind of restaurant along the way. We would drive only about 150 mile per day as my car would only go about 45 miles per hour, so our trip was quire leisurely.

It was summer and warm even in the Upper Peninsula so we took off one morning, taking highway 21 east to Grand Rapids, then highway US 131 north to Kalkaska, a small town about 170 miles distant. There we found a small restaurant and a tourist camp where we stopped for the night. Our room was a separate small wooden cabin with a bare light bulb hanging from the ceiling. There was a double bed, a chest of drawers, a table, and two straight chairs. After a quick supper at the restaurant, we went to bed early, about nine o'clock. We got up early and washed up at the tourist camp wash room apart from the cabins where the toilets and lavatories were. There were no bathtubs or showers.

We kept the top up the whole way on the trip. An occasional shower didn't bother us too much. If there was a heavy rain, we stopped and fastened on the side curtains. This took about half an hour and was a job requiring patience and muscle to get them to fit. We only did this twice.

We kept going northward on US 131 to Petosky, then US 31 to Mackinaw City, the Straits of Mackinac and the ferry to St. Ignace, a distance of ninety miles. We were the first car to drive on the car ferry so that we were at the far end and ours would be the first car to drive off the boat at St. Ignace. The ferry took about an hour. When we got to the dock and the barrier was taken down in front of my car, I stepped on the starter and nothing happened. I sprang out of the driver's seat, lifted the wood floor-board and uncovered the battery. Sure enough, a couple of firm blows with my trusty wood hammer on the cable connections to the battery posts were enough so that when I jumped back into the car and stomped on the starter button, the engine turned over and quickly started. I gave thanks to the Patron Saint of Teen-Age Boys Driving Cars That Belonged in a Junk Yard when the engine came to life, and we drove off the ferry boast with a couple of dozen cars impatiently waiting for us to get out of the way. Don Jerrems was impressed. He said he never would have known what to do to start the car.

The distance from Saint Ignace to The Soo was about fifty miles. We were stopped on the Canadian side where a uniformed guard at the entrance asked us who we were, what were we going to do in Canada, where were we staying, and for how long. We seemed to give him the right answers as he waved us on after a few minutes.

We found a sort of guest house with a sign in front saying, "Tourists Welcome." We were given a bedroom on the second floor with the bathroom down the hall. Six dollars per night for the two of us. It was late afternoon in the town of Sault Saint Marie and when we walked from our guest house a couple of blocks to the main street, we could see that the main businesses of this Canadian community on the United States border during Prohibition were beer taverns and stores selling bottled alcoholic beverages. There were throngs of what we figured were Americans who came for brief visits to drink. Don Jerrems and I were not thinking about drinking beer as we probably would not have been served anyway, but we went into a few taverns as innocent curiosity-seekers and ordered ginger ale. Most taverns were crowded with noisy but well-behaved men, a few accompanied by women.

We left the next morning after having dinner and breakfast at the guest house, another dollar-fifty each. We found that everyone in town preferred United States dollars. Coming back we had to take US #2 from The Soo to Saint Ignace, but we then took US #27 through Cheboygan on Lake Huron and it carried us south through Wolverine, Grayling, and Mount Pleasant to a junction with Michigan #21 west to Grand Rapids and Holland. We stopped one night at Mount Pleasant where we found a private home that accepted tourists. This was our best overnight stay with kind people, a clean, comfortable bedroom, and dinner and breakfast. We were now about 140 miles from Castle Park. We left in mid-morning and after stopping for lunch in Grand

Rapids, we drove through Zeeland and Holland and arrived at the Castle in mid afternoon.

We had been away four days and our money was about gone but we had seen a small part of Canada and a larger part of northern Michigan, all in pleasant summer weather. I let Don drive a lot of the way back as he now knew the limitations of my car and would not demand more or it. We had become trusting friends with mutual respect beneath the usual veneer of teen-age cynicism and we never had a disagreement that was not quickly resolved.

THE FINAL TRAGEDY

The summer passed quickly after our Canadian trip and I did not attempt any more dates with the Castle Park girls except for a few casual daytime rides in my car to the beach or to Macatawa. After Labor Day, families began to leave Castle Park after spending a full summer. These departures had become ritual events, observed with some ceremony. When it became known that a family was leaving, there would be at least a few other remaining family members gathered in front of the Castle under the large oak tree there with the departing family all loaded up, usually in an open touring car, with the children waving goodbye and exchanging hugs. When the car pulled away, the ritual goodbye cheer was "Ricket racket! Zicket zacket! Siss boom bah! Castle Park, Castle Park, Rah, rah, rah! Ice Cream and soda water, Ginger ale and pop! Castle Park, Castle Park, always on the top! Y-E-A-A-Y!" After that the car would drive off with everybody waving goodbye. Doctor Jay was a frequent semi-organizer of these departure ceremonies. He was a thin, aceticlooking, chain-smoking physician from St. Louis and long-term Castle Parker who would spread the word that a particular family was "leaving in the morning, so let's be there to see them off," and lead the departing cheer.

Our family stayed until mid-September and departed one morning in our four-door Buick sedan with the usual goodbye cheers in front of the Castle. I departed the same day a little later without any cheers from anybody, alone in my car and ready for the adventure of going 150 miles on US #31 to Chicago. This trip was uneventful, but when I reached 72nd Street near the lake and the entrance to the South Shore Country Club, I decided to drive in to see if anybody I knew was there and to get some lunch. I was ravenously hungry at two o'clock in the afternoon.

I found my friend, Al Nowack, in one of the outdoor dining areas and he told me to order what I wanted. I had a large beef sandwich and some iced tea and felt much better. He charged it to his father as he knew I was not allowed to charge it to mine. I went on home after that and was busy for a day or two getting ready for the year at school.

The following Saturday afternoon, I was in my car on Stony Island Avenue going toward the 59th Street entrance to Jackson Park. The avenue had double street-car track with the cars going in both directions. I was in the right-hand lane at 59th Street, headed south with a streetcar behind me going in the same direction. When it passed me on my left, I turned sharply left to go into

Jackson Park but I didn't see another streetcar coming in the opposite direction at thirty miles an hour. BANG! It made a horrible crunching noise as it hit the right rear of my car, knocking it off the track and turning it around facing in the opposite direction from the streetcar. My car was totally disabled in this glancing collision, but all it did was shake me up. I got out of the driver's seat uninjured but in total shock and my heart beating wildly. The motorman got out of the streetcar and without any unnecessary conversation asked me if I was hurt, took my name and address, gave me his badge number, wrote down my license number, helped me push my car over to the curb on the left, got back in his streetcar, and went on down Stony Island Avenue at thirty miles an hour. His load of passengers looked on with mixed expressions of boredom and impatience when they realized that this was just a minor accident with no casualties.

I was devastated because my car was badly smashed on the right rear with that wheel crushed and that whole part of the body pushed completely out of shape. It was undriveable and a total loss. I climbed into the driver's seat and sat awhile until I could calm down. I loved that car. It was *my car* and now I had let somebody hurt it, which was the same as hurting *me*, and it was all my fault because I was careless. As Adlai Stevenson once said, "I'm too big to cry, and it hurts too much to laugh."

I sat there in the driver's seat of my demolished car for about twenty minutes, thinking of what to do. I finally decided to do the thing I least wanted, which was to call my father. I got out of the car, walked to a nearby delicatessen on Stony Island Avenue where I knew there was a phone, and I called home where my father always was on Saturdays. He took the news quite well and appeared to be concerned about any possible injury to me. When he learned that my car was a total loss, it may have been a welcome piece of news for I had heard him say more than once that high-school boys shouldn't have cars. He considered my car to be a sort of summertime adventure, not to be continued through the school year. He asked me if I could walk home and I said yes. He said, "Do that. I'll have your car picked up and taken away." He called Clyde Warner, a special friend whom he saw every Sunday at church. Clyde Warner was a contradiction in terms, a church-going, quietly and sincerely religious used-car salesman and part owner of a garage. He and his partner, Tom Kadlac, owned the garage and a used-car lot. Tom was a mechanic who ran the garage and was usually found with his head under the hood of a car doing an engine job. Clyde was out on the used-car lot and had a record of selling more cars than anybody in that part of the city. It was said that he told the truth about his products, a trait not thought of as being common among used-car salesmen. He and Tom also had a wrecker, a tow truck that they used to bring in damaged cars like mine.

There were several occasions when Clyde Warner would come to Sunday dinner at our house at the invitation of my father. He was a widower and my father probably perceived him to be leading a lonely life on weekends, so he came to our house, looking as he did all week long, like a tall, gray-haired, distinguished New York banker dressed in an expensive blue suit, a white shirt with a detachable stiff collar, a dark necktie with a large diamond stick-pin in it, and a vest with a long heavy watch-chain spread between its lower pockets. He treated everybody, including me, with great dignity.

My father, being equally devoted to the Presbyterian Church and all its Calvinism and predestination, had Mr. Warner come for Sunday dinner because he thought it would be a good example for us to be exposed to a guest who shared my father's fundamentalist religious beliefs. When my father phoned him to tell him my sad story, Mr. Warner arranged with Tom Kadlac to send the tow-truck over to Stony Island Avenue to pick up my car and take it away. I waited until it came, after assuring policemen in a passing open Lincoln squad car that I was indeed waiting for a tow-truck to remove the car. Finally, the wrecker came and I watched as my car was hoisted up by its front wheels and hauled off to a junkyard on Halsted Street. I watched it go away and take with it a measure of my freedom and an end to romance and adventure. It was the final curtain on a tragedy of Shakespearean magnitude. I was not to own another car until fourteen years later.

BACKYARD BASEBALL

Like most of the pre-teen boys growing up in Hyde Park in Chicago, baseball was something we all played, beginning in the spring before going away to Michigan for the summer. We played in Jackman Field behind our elementary school during a compulsory gym period every afternoon.

But the real adjustment of baseball's rules to accommodate special conditions came when we played in the backyard of the Stevens boys' home on 58th Street near the school. There are many forms of baseball from the big league version to the pick-up sandlot modifications. The ability of baseball to adapt itself was tested by four boys and a dog in 1927. The rules were set out by three brothers and me, so that our game would be clarified and disciplined.

Baseball adjusted to our self-made regulations because baseball is different from other games in that it is not limited by time; it is outside of time. Theoretically, a game can go on forever. We found that we had to make our own rules, and, in the case of a disagreement about the outcome of a play, in the absence of an umpire we would toss a coin to come to the final decision.

Here are the rules, which provided for competition between two teams of two players:

1. Underhand easy pitching.
2. Indian ball.
3. Pitcher's hands are out.
4. Over the fence is out.
5. If a player is on base and a hit is made, the player must go home. If home plate is touched by an opposing player holding the ball, the player on base is out.
6. If there is any dispute, a coin must be tossed to determine the decision.
7. If the ball hits Monday on a doubtful play, the play goes over.
8. A player on base can go as far as possible on any out, except a strikeout.
9. On June 10, provided that more than 15 five-inning games have been played, and provided that one team is more than one game ahead of the other team, the losing team must buy for the winning team all the sodas, ice cream, malted milks, and sundaes that the winning team can eat in one hour at Kuenster's Drugstore on 57th Street.

Signed
(s) Bill Stevens   (s) John Stevens
(s) Sam Hair (s) Jim Stevens

It is well to explain that rule number seven refers to "Monday", a large black and tan collie dog, who would play if he could, but we told him he was not in the lineup. He was free to run and bark, and participate in that way in the excitement of the game.

The deadline of June 10th was established because that was about the time when we all went away to Michigan for the summer: the Stevens boys to Lakeside, and I to Castle park, not to return until after Labor Day.

It didn't matter that there were only two on each team. And rule number four–"Over the fence is out"–provided our adjustment to baseball's spatial frame, which projects the lines from home plate to first and third bases into infinity. Any ball hit within that ultimate projection is fair; outside those lines it is foul, but sometimes playable. But we had outfield limits imposed by a fence, two brick walls, and one large house surrounding the back yard playing field.

Baseball being a game of records, it is unfortunate that there are no records of the scores of these games, and the names of those on the winning team are lost forever in the mists of over three score and ten years. The players survive: Two of the brothers are retired lawyers. The third and the youngest brother is also a lawyer, and at this writing is an Associate Justice of the United States Supreme Court. I am the fourth player, not a lawyer, but carrying with me the confirmation of the metaphysical nature of our national pastime, and now more than ever aware that baseball ignores time. We proved it long ago.

A POSTSCRIPT TO THE NAKED NAVY

There were five of us in the boyhood Naked Navy at Castle Park, all within a year of each other in age, and inseparable for several summers when we did everything together.

Fifteen years later, after Pearl Harbor, we were all in the military. At war's end, we all came home, except one. Johnny Needham was our only hero.

After graduating from Harvard in 1936, he took some post-graduate courses, then went on a European trip with a friend in the summer of 1938. On his return, he told his friends and family that there were ominous preparations for war in Europe, particularly by the Germans. In the summer of 1940, he joined the Navy V-7 program for line officer training. He was commissioned as an ensign in February 1941, and ordered to Shanghai for duty aboard the *Luzon*, a river-patrol boat in the Yangtze. In November, to escape the Japanese, the *Luzon* sailed for Manila, arriving December 4th. In subsequent action in Manila Bay, the *Luzon* was sunk by Japanese aircraft. The ship's crew survived to escape to Corregidor, and were there when General Wainright surrendered on May 6th, 1942.

John was one of many sent to the infamous Japanese prison camp at Cabanatuan. Life there for two and a half years was a struggle for survival and for sanity under the harsh and senselessly cruel punishments imposed by the Japanese guards.

MacArthur returned to the Philippines in October, 1944, coming ashore at Leyte. By December, the Japanese were in full retreat, evacuating all prisoners for shipment to Japan. 1600 prisoners were taken from Cabanatuan and placed aboard the *Oryoku Maru*, an unmarked freighter. It did not get far; it was sunk by Navy TBF's in Subic Bay. Many, including John, survived and were able to swim ashore to be recaptured by the Japanese, then reshipped from San Fernando in northern Luzon on another unmarked freighter, the *Enoura Maru*. This ship got as far as the coast of Formosa, about 400 nautical miles north of Luzon, where a direct bomb hit from a Navy plane killed nearly all those in the forward hold, including John. The bodies were taken ashore and burned.

There are 17,206 military men and women buried at the *Manila American Cemetery and Memorial*. Another 36,279 names, including that of *NEEDHAM John C., Ensign, USNR Illinois*, are inscribed on what are described as *The Walls of Memory*. So, our boyhood group at Castle Park produced one hero: he survived two and a half years of Japanese inhumanity in a prison camp; then, the unintended tragedy was that we took his life away, But we didn't mean to. Humanum est errare.

II. CLIFTON

THE OLD HOMESTEAD

Sometimes instead of going to Castle Park for the entire summer, we would go to Grandmother Cummings' home in Clifton, about ninety miles south of Chicago. It was and still is a small town of about 400 people near the Indiana border and on the main line of the Illinois Central Railroad, which went west and south from Chicago to Cairo, Illinois and to New Orleans. Briefly in the 1850s, it was the longest railroad in the world, soon to be surpassed by others going west from Chicago to California.

Grandfather Cummings died a few months before I was born so I never saw him, but I was named for him and later in my life, reading his obituaries, I knew he must have been an important figure in Iroquois County. He owned grain elevators in seven towns on the railroad and eleven farms comprising 3500 acres of the wonderfully fertile Illinois corn land. The "corn belt" began in western Ohio and went west through Indiana, Illinois, Iowa, and eastern Nebraska.

When he died in 1914, my grandmother, as executor, wanted my father to be the manager of the estate and all its properties and assets. This was at least partly because she thought there was no one else among the older employees of the grain company whom she could trust with the responsibility. As the husband of one of her daughters, she thought she could trust her favorite son-in-law. So, he was persuaded to leave his job as one of the leading young executives at the Acme Steel Products Company in Chicago and to open an office at 20 West Jackson Boulevard as vice-president and general manager of the R. F. Cummings Estate. He and his secretary, Miss Stockholm, were there until 1935. After that, when the consequences of Mr. Cummings' highly leveraged borrowing habits began to cause serious difficulty in making mortgage payments on the farms, combined with the price of corn that had fallen to forty cents per bushel in 1935, my father could only stem the losses to the estate as best he could. He was finally compelled to sell some of the farms or let the lenders take them back. Four of them remained intact and clear of debt. These were the farms inherited by my mother, her two sisters Lenore and Marian, and her brother Marston. By 1935, the exigencies of the Great Depression made them cash out and, against my father's advice, they sold their farms at deep discounts. My mother was the exception. She had inherited "Shore Woods," a beautiful piece of farm land on the Iroquois River near Ashkum, Illinois, about four miles east of Clifton. She never relinquished title to this property and when my father retired thirty years later, it became one of their main sources of support.

The house in Clifton was known in our family as "The Old Homestead." My mother said it was built in 1879 by her grandfather, S. K. Marston, who lived in Onarga, a nearby town in Iroquois County. He was a native of Maine and a founding member of the "Connecticut Colony," a group of families who came to Illinois in the 1850s and settled in Onarga. He was also a master builder.

Mr. Cummings told his father-in-law to "draw the plans, and don't bother me with the details. Leave that to Minnie (my grandmother)." They wanted to have the biggest house in Clifton with the living room, dining room, kitchen, and master bedroom on the first floor, five bedrooms upstairs and a wide porch on the front and one side. As originally built, there was no plumbing. The biggest house in Clifton had a two-hole privy outside near the back kitchen door. About a year later, two full bathrooms were added, one upstairs and one down.

Each bedroom had a washstand with a pitcher sitting in a large washbowl. The pitcher would be filled with hot water every morning by a young girl servant living in the house, who did some cleaning, helped in the kitchen, and was a nanny to the children. Underneath each bed was a chamber-pot for use when necessary at night and provided a reprieve from a trip to the outdoor privy.

In the living room was the square grand piano that had been a part of Grandmother Cummings' life for so many years. There was also a little table in one corner for a phonograph that played cylinders. The selection of cylinders, kept in a shelf under the phonograph, was limited to a few renditions of country and classical. Those that I remember and would occasionally play were "Buffalo Gal," "The Prisoner's Song," "The Wreck Of The Old 97," "The Yellow Rose Of Texas," and "After The Ball." I listened to these tinny and scratchy recordings over and over, memorizing all the words.

The stove in the kitchen was a huge wood-burner with a large tank attached behind it, the source of hot water. The sink had a pump handle at one end that pumped rain water out of the cistern underneath the dining room floor. The cistern was fed by rainwater and a system of gutters, downspouts, and pipes from the eaves on the roof. If it didn't rain for more than a week, there was no water in the cistern and water was fetched to the kitchen in pails filled from a pump in the back yard.

The water we used from the pump and from the cistern was probably a lot purer than the milk we drank. That came from the Jersey cow in a nearby pasture and barn belonging to a friend and neighbor who kept his own cow there. An arrangement was made for some kind of reciprocal agreement that compensated the neighbor. It was probably a payment of rent for the pasture and the care of our cow.

In my grandmother's home, there was almost always an Irish teen-age girl who lived in the house and became, for a few years, a member of the family. These girls came mainly from the farms. When they were into their middle teens, many of them wanted to continue their schooling in Kanakee, or perhaps move to Chicago for jobs in the offices and factories there.

That area of Iroquois County, and more generally of the entire corn belt, was becoming inhabited by many of Western European origins, including Belgians, Germans, French, Irish, many of them Catholic. They supported the beautiful church at L'Erable, a village a few miles north of Clifton established by French settlers many years before.

At the end of every afternoon in Clifton, the *Chicago Daily News* would be delivered to our home by Neal, who would toss it up on the front steps and blow his whistle to let us know the paper was there. Neal rode a bike with a basket on the back, delivering the paper every day except Sunday. The morning paper, the *Chicago Tribune*, came on the morning train from Chicago. A bundle of about twenty papers would be tossed off on the station platform as the train went through. Lou Vansant would walk over to the station and pick up a copy for the grain company office. But somehow it was more soothing to hear Neal's whistle at the end of the day and have the *Chicago Daily* News delivered to our doorstep. In the absence of radio and television, we knew that it would tell us all we needed to know about the world outside of Clifton.

THE BYFORDS

Harry Byford lived behind our Clifton homestead and was a long-time employee of the grain company. His little two-story house adjoined our back yard and Mrs. Byford was my dear friend when I was little. They had one daughter, Vivian, who was older than I and ignored me with studied indifference. Harry ran the stationary engine at the grain elevator that powered the hoists that lifted the corn up to the tops of the bins. He also drove the seven-passenger Willys touring car on some weekends when we would go out to visit the farms or to have a picnic on a Sunday at my mother's farm on the river. Harry was big, gnarled, and bony with huge hands and resembled somewhat a beardless Lincoln. He had an inquisitive look as if he wanted to understand events around him and spoke only when spoken to. Mrs. Byford helped my grandmother in the kitchen and worked in the garden behind her house. I never knew her first name, whereas everyone called her husband Harry.

Their daughter, Vivian, grew up to be a beautiful, dark-haired slender teen-age graduate of the high school in Clifton. She then went off to Chicago to study at a business school. My mother, as tactfully as she could, often asked Mrs. Byford about Vivian. Mrs. Byford would say she hadn't heard form Vivian and sometimes would burst into tears as she said so. It became accepted that Vivian was never heard from except indirectly or by chance when someone from Clifton would be in Chicago and hear about her. Ten years later she was reported to be happily married and living in Downer's Grove, a western suburb of Chicago. She never made any effort to communicate with her Clifton parents or childhood friends.

THE ELEVATOR

At harvest time in September and October, the farmers would bring in their corn in horse drawn wagons and park the wagons on the scale next to the grain company office to be weighed. Then they drove the team across the road to the elevator entrance that was a slight upward grade into the interior. When the wagon was still tilted a little backward inside the elevator, blocks were put behind the rear wheels and the rear section of the wagon lifted to let the corn fall down into the bin that had been opened in the floor behind the wagon. This was corn on the cob. The wonderful mechanical combine machine was not yet perfected, which in later years would go through a cornfield and shelled corn would come shooting out of its spout into a truck alongside. The horse-drawn wagons would then proceed through the elevator and circle around back to the scale to be weighed again empty. The farmer would be handed a receipt showing the amount of corn in that load and now in the elevator. On some October days, dozens of wagons would go through the process in Clifton and in the other elevators in the seven towns along the railroad operated by the R. F. Cummings Grain Co.

As a small boy, I found it fascinating to watch this procedure with the horses straining to pull the loaded wagons up the slope of the elevator entrance and then come rapidly out the other end with the harnesses jingling and the wagons creaking and rattling. They were mostly dark green and all of a size. The horses and their harnesses all looked as if they came from the same source. When they weren't pulling the wagons, the horses were used for plowing. It was not until the 1940s in that part of Illinois that the tractor replaced the horse at the plow and the wagons began to be replaced by trucks.

MY CHORE

We spent parts of some summers in the 1920s in Clifton from mid-June to mid-July. Then we'd make the long drive to Castle Park, about 200 miles over narrow, two-lane concrete roads. During the month that we were in Clifton, there was always a crowd in The Old Homestead-our whole family of five and frequent guests, usually friends from Chicago. I spent parts of every day with the Sheldon boys, Henry and Bub, who lived about a block away and behind us. They were close to me in age, part of a family that included two older sisters, an older brother, and two dogs. The boys had a coaster wagon like mine called American Flyers. They could be pulled with a tiller or I could kneel on my left knee in the wagon, steer it with the tiller pulled back with my left hand and propel it with my right leg. This could be done only on the few cement sidewalks in town. I got to know every crack in every sidewalk from our house to the stores on the main street.

When I was seven, my wagon and I were given an important responsibility. My mother wrote down a grocery list to be taken to the A. L. Morel & Son store on the main street across the railroad from the grain company office. She pinned the list to my shirt and told me to go with my wagon to the store and give the list to Mr. Morel. I was to bring everything back in my American Flyer. I was, by this time, very proficient in propelling my wagon on the sidewalks with my right leg, avoiding the cracks and developing some speed.

So, on several mornings during the month we were in Clifton, I would go to the Morel General Store, or sometimes with another list to the Beardslee-Sanderson Drygoods Store. On these errands when I reached the grain company office next to the railroad, Lou Vansant, the manager, or Millie Reid, the bookkeeper, would come out and see me across the tracks. I considered this to be totally unnecessary. I told my mother I had sense enough not to go across railroad track if a train was coming, but she would phone ahead and tell "Uncle Lou" to watch for me anyway.

When my mission was completed, Mr. Morel would see me across the railroad track and I had to pull the loaded wagon all the way home where I delivered everything to the back door and into the kitchen. This made me feel that I had contributed to the survival of our family and , that now they would find it difficult to live without me and my American Flyer. My mother also gave me extra cookies.

III. ROCKY MOUNTAIN NATIONAL PARK

JACK MOOMAW

Jack Moomaw was my hero. Like many of the year-round rangers at Rocky Mountain National Park in the 1930s, he was a Colorado native and a World War I veteran. Jack was a stubby, round-faced man with reddish hair, never combed. He wore his uniform coat open all the time, except when he was talking to Ed Rogers, the park superintendent. Then he would make a concession to authority by wiping off his boots and getting all buttoned up, even though his side pockets were bulging like saddle bags with pipes, tobacco, nails, papers, and miscellaneous small tools he might need. Usually, he had a pipe clenched in his mouth with a curved stem and the bowl hanging down on his chin. Jack once came off of a pack trip of several days in a foul humor because he had run out of pipe tobacco. I offered him a cigarette and he took one look at it and said "Nah!" with great contempt. I went straight to Koontz's store near my campground and bought him a tin of Prince Albert so he could roll his own. I was told that he was of French descent, although he didn't look like it, and that his real name was Jacques Meaumeaux. He looked much more Irish to me.

He had been with the Park Service since 1920 and when I knew him he was about forty. He referred to his wife as "that woman." It's true she usually looked disheveled and harassed, but always greeted me nicely and took an interest in me. She had a way of looking at me in a motherly way and asking how I was getting along. I always said I was doing just fine, thanks, and she would look at me again, skeptically. She had long stringy yellow hair, wore shapeless gingham dresses, and was always working at cleaning up their little house near Estes Park. This was because Jack left a trail behind him of dirty ashtrays and clothes thrown down on chairs and tables. They had a pretty daughter named Pattie who looked just like a smaller version of her mother but Pattie's long blond hair was never stringy and she moved with great grace. She was fourteen and a tomboy. She rode horses all summer and skied all winter and wondered why she couldn't go out at night with the boys she rode and skied with.

I was in charge of a campground, Aspenglen, north of Estes Park and near the Fall River entrance. There was a one-room cabin there for me, a one-hole wood stove, a table, a straight chair, some shelves, and a cupboard next to the stove. The park service furnished a frying pan, a coffee pot, a kettle, three metal bowls, some chipped china plates, metal cups, a few knives, forks and spoons, and one Coleman gasoline lantern. There was an iron bunk bed with a thin mattress and no bedding. I bought a pillow and four surplus army blankets in Estes Park and slept without sheets. I did not consider this a hardship but the bed had to be neatly made each morning when Jack usually appeared at eight o'clock to see if I was alive and well. There was no electricity, no refrigerator, no water. The campground had four outhouses, two each for men and women. Each had four holes. I was to keep them swept out and supplied with toilet paper. There was one faucet about ten feet from my cabin where I could get water. It was also for the campers on that side of the campground. There was another faucet about fifty yards away. This was all the water available for forty campsites, but it was not looked upon then as being inadequate.

In those Depression years, entire families from Iowa, Nebraska, Kansas, and Oklahoma would come to Aspenglen, pitch tents, and spend the summer. Some of the members were teachers on vacation. Other families would pass through and spend a night, a week, or a month. Mornings, I would be out-of-uniform and in my work clothes and cowboy boots, hauling trash in a wheelbarrow and answering dozens of questions about birds, flowers, trees, and ground animals. I also ate many meals of all descriptions with various campers and found it better than trying to cook for myself. I ate very well. I made coffee in the morning and maybe ate some breakfast food, but lunch could be just about anywhere I chose among the campers and I would be included as a sought-after guest if I turned up as they were getting the meal ready.

It was raining heavily one evening and I was in my cabin reading the *Biological Sciences Syllabus,* as I had to take an exam when I got back to school in late September. Jack Moomaw's personal car was a Ford Model A roadster, a two seater with a rumble seat and a soft top. He had the side curtains fastened on. He drove up and banged on my door. When I let him in, he said "Come on, we're going to Denver. Get your uniform on." I didn't understand about the uniform because I sensed this was an off-duty trip, but I put it on while he sat on the bed and waited impatiently. He asked if I had any whisky and I answered that I had a pint. He said, 'That's enough. Bring it with you." This was only a few weeks after I had started work at Apenglen and didn't really know Jack's habits or motivations. When I was ready, we got into the car and started down the Big Thompson road to Denver. As soon as we got into the car, Jack pulled out his own pint of whisky and passed it to me. We passed it back and forth and it was gone by the time we had gone thirty miles.

I had no idea where we were going in Denver. I didn't ask. I was nineteen-years-old, this was my first real job with anybody and this was my boss I was with. My attitude toward him was one of total respect and fear.

We drove into the city and Jack seemed to know exactly where to go. It was a side street with retail storefronts, closed up and dark. He stopped and parked on the street where there were just a few cars parked in a space of several blocks. It was now about nine o'clock. There was an unmarked doorway next to one of the storefronts. We opened this door and went up a flight of dimly-lit stairs to the second floor. At the landing there was a heavy door on the left, painted red with a large brass knocker and a doorbell. Shortly after Jack rang the bell, a slot in the middle of the door opened and a woman's voice said, "Who is it?"

Jack said, "Hey, it's me, Shirley." She unbolted the door and let us in. "Who's your friend?"

"He's Sam, He works for me and he's all right."

"Okay, Hi, Sam." She gave me a big smile.

I felt that she accepted me. She had probably once been beautiful and was still an attractive woman with a full figure and long dark hair, pulled behind her ears with a ribbon. She wore an expensive blue dress with an orange belt. She had on little makeup. Her expression was cheerful, her dark eyes lighting up with her animated manner. I could tell she was fully in charge. I knew now that Jack Moomaw had brought me to a Denver bordello, both of us in full uniform. I didn't know how to behave.

We went into the small anteroom about ten feet square with a hall going off to the right of the front door. There was a large table next to the wall opposite the front door. At each end of the table there was a wicker armchair with a cushioned seat. Two other side chairs were against the wall to the left. On the table was a large lamp, about two feet high, with a heavy circular base. Standing on the base was the figure of a nude young woman with her head turned to one shoulder and with her opposite arm held up over her head, her hand holding the lamp assembly to the light, the light switch and the wire holder for the lampshade. The lampshade was a dark yellow translucent plastic with black line drawings all around it showing a man and a woman in a dozen different positions of sexual intercourse. With the lamp turned on, these became quite vivid and graphic

It was now about ten o'clock. Two girls came down the hall into the anteroom. They wore only loose shifts. We were apparently the only customers that night. One girl was a sort of ash blonde, taller than the other, who was petite and dark. Jack pulled another pint bottle out of his pocket and put it on the table with the lamp. "How about some glasses and ginger ale, Shirley." he said. She went back down the hall and reappeared shortly with three glasses, a large bottle of ginger ale, and a dish of ice on a tray. The girls were young, no more than twenty, probably younger. They were laughing and working at being companionable. Jack poured two fingers of whiskey into a glass and drank it neat without offering any to anyone. Shirley said it was too late for the girls to have another drink. To me, she said, "Can I fix you one?"

"Yes, please, but mostly ginger ale." By this time, after a two-hour drive to Denver, I had probably had the better part of pint of whiskey straight out of the bottle. My ears were ringing. I could walk and talk, but it was an effort.

"Come on, Betty." said Jack, motioning to the blonde and taking off his coat. They went to one of the rooms.

"Well, Sam?" Shirley said.

"My name's Brenda," said the small brunette. I was nothing if not polite. I tried to think of a way to delay the next most obvious turn of events. I turned away from Brenda and looked at Shirley. I said, "I feel terrible, my ears are ringing. We've been drinking whisky all the way from Estes Park. I don't think I can do anything."

She said, "Okay, I understand. Come on back to the kitchen and I'll fix you a cup of really black coffee. You can come back here some other time when you're feeling better." Mostly, I wanted to get out of there as quickly as possible.

A lot of "what ifs" came to my mind. What if the chief ranger found out I was running up to Denver to a house of ill-fame in uniform after a month on the job? Other "what ifs" involved my father, a God-fearing Calvinistic Presbyterian who was responsible for getting me this job because he knew Secretary of the Interior Ickes.

We went back to the kitchen and I sat at the table while Shirley made the coffee and I told her I was in college in Chicago and I hoped she wasn't mad at me. She said of course she wasn't and don't worry about it. She said she saw Jack pretty regularly every couple of months, always alone. "He must trust you." When, after about twenty minutes of conversation, we went back to the front room, the two girls had disappeared, Jack was nowhere to be seen, and the lamp on the table was gone. Shirley was quiet for a moment then she said, "Goddammit, Sam, your friend has stolen my lamp!" She became quite excited, went to the front window overlooking the street, opened it, and could see Jack sitting in his car. She shouted, "All right, Jack, you can bring back that lamp. Sam stays here until you do. And you know I can call the cops if I want to! I'll give you five minutes!" She slammed the window shut.

We could see Jack climb slowly out of the car, lift the lamp out of the rumble seat, and bring it up the stairs. "I was going to pay you for it," he said to Shirley.

"Well, you owe me twenty-five dollars."

"I thought it was twenty dollars."

"Five bucks extra for sobering up your friend and for you trying to steal my lamp."

I collected myself and said, "Thanks, Shirley. I guess we'll go now." Jack handed her the money and we went down the stairs to his car. He drove to the outskirts of Denver, stopped the car at a closed-up gas station, and said, "Do you feel like driving?"

"Okay."

So we traded places and I drove the rest of the way with Jack snoring peacefully beside me. We got to Aspenglen at about four A.M. and Jack dropped me off without a word. The next morning he came by at eight o'clock as usual to see if I was up and working. I was, and he said nothing about the previous evening then or at any other time for the next three years. We both knew I wouldn't say anything to anybody about it.

I didn't until years later when we had a sort of reunion at Grand Lake of a few of the 1930s temporary rangers and Jack had been dead for ten years. I told everybody how Jack Moomaw had been instrumental in having me held hostage in a Denver cat house, an event which didn't appear in the autobiographical reminiscences he published called *My Recollections As A Rocky Mountain Ranger*, but which remains with me as a cherished memory of an impossibly bizarre event, beyond all reproach by my father, the National Park Service, or the Secretary of the Interior.

Jack accomplished much in his career in the Park Service. A memorable achievement was the installation of cables on the steep, rocky path up the north face of Long's Peak to aid those ascending. The cables remained for fifty years until 1973 when Long's Peak was given wilderness designation and the cables were removed. Jack was also the first to make a recorded January climb of Long's Peak in 1922. To be first, he made the ascent New Years' Eve, 1921, in the dark. He had none of today's mountaineering equipment, but used a hatchet to pound in his pitons and to chop his way through snow and ice. *The Estes Park Trail* described this as "almost superhuman."

Patty Moomaw, Jack and Lila's daughter, born in 1925, was Jack's pride and joy. With his tutelage, she became the Colorado high school skiing champion, and, in 1941, was crowned "Rooftop Rodeo Queen." She attended Colorado State university, graduating in 1946; she then married a boyhood friend, Forrest Button. They had a daughter, Helen Lila. Patty died suddenly in 1947 of a cerebral hemorrhage. Jack and Lila were devastated; Jack never emotionally recovered. Lila mailed me a short note in December 1948, in response to a Christmas card I had sent them. All it said was, "Thank you, Sam, for your kind remembrance. Patty passed away last winter. Jack and Lila." That was the first I had heard about it.

Over the years, Jack wrote several books of poetry and memoirs, and was a self educated authority on Colorado Native American archeology. He retired from the Park Service in 1948, after 23 years, and lived mostly in Lyons, Colorado, pursuing his various hobbies and literary pursuits until his death from a heart attack in 1974 at 82. He was a strange, hard-living, opinionated, marvelously diversified man. I'm glad I knew him.

GRAND LAKE

Fred McLaren was the district ranger on the eastern slope of the continental Divide in rocky Mountain notional Park at the Grand Lake Ranger Station. He was, as were several others on the ranger staff, a veteran of the First World War and probably was assisted in obtaining the job as a result of veteran's preference. He had no higher education but had been in the Colorado mountains all his life, except for his time in the army in France. He learned how to ski as a boy before it became a popular sport because it was frequently the only way of getting from one place to another during the winter. He knew all about horses, the fundamentals of carpentry, how to fix most plumbing, and was a shade-tree auto mechanic. Most of all, he was good natured, could be firm when he had to be, would try to understand both sides of an argument, and was gifted with great patience in handling his "90-day wonder" temporary rangers, myself among them. He needed this patience with me because I did not know how to do anything involving horses, carpentry, plumbing, or much else for that matter of a practical nature. Whatever I might have learned in school or at the university was now completely irrelevant in this place, in this job.

Fred had a wife named Iva, who was larger than he was and probably stronger. She was kind and gentle and like Fred, was firm when she had to be while raising a family of three boys and two girls. Bert was the youngest, about four, Dick and Doug were the next oldest, then Dorothy and Sarah. Fred's production of a new child in his family nearly every year earned him the friendly nick-name of "Sure-Shot McLaren" among his Grand Lake friends. The McLarens lived in a large frame house just outside the park near the town of Grand Lake. They had a cow in the barn that the boys would milk every day and then put out to graze. There was a corral with four horses belonging to the Park Service and a stable with all the saddlery, blankets, and other gear for the care of the horses. At the ranger station at the Grand Lake Entrance where we lived, there were two pick-up trucks and a flatbed on which was mounted a gasoline engine that ran a pump with 300 feet of hose for use in fighting small forest fires when the truck could be driven to within about a hundred feet of a source of water. We were seldom invited to Fred's home, but Iva could be depended on to sew on any buttons that came off my uniforms and to talk to me in a friendly way to see if I was getting along all right. There were three of us living in the 15x15 wood cabin at the Grand Lake Entrance and in there were two double-deck bunk beds with thin mattresses, a table with four straight chairs, a wood-burning two-lid stove for heating and cooking, and a shelf below a window with a pan for water and a mirror. No plumbing, no icebox. there was a privy out in back and a faucet near the front door for water. The mornings were cold, about forty degrees. Sometimes we would prepare a fire in the stove with paper and kindling, leave the lid off, sprinkle a cup of gasoline on it, then throw lighted kitchen matches at it in the morning until at would start with a small explosion and soon take the chill off so we could get out of bed and get dressed. Breakfast was usually orange juice, cold cereal, and milk. Each of us had specific jobs. One was to check in every car coming through the entrance from 8 A.M. to 5 P.M. Another was to go to McLaren's stable, saddle a horse and ride up the various half-dozen trails to check campers, picnickers, hikers and others, each trail on a different day. My job was highway patrol.

Fred knew that I didn't know much about the outdoors, but I could probably drive a small truck, so I was provided with a five-year-old Chevy pickup that had been painted with the NPS green and the RMNP emblem. It had been fitted with a siren next to the left front headlight that could be turned on by a switch on the steering column. This was a time of reduced budgets in the 1930s for the national parks and much had to be done with equipment already at hand. The Chevy truck didn't look like a patrol car but that's what it was. My job was to see that the 35mph speed limit wasn't exceeded too much, to stop anybody seen throwing trash on the highways, or anybody driving recklessly. There were several parking areas between Grand Lake and the top of the Fall River Pass and I would stop at these with some regularity to answer the inevitable questions. I would be asked to name a particular flower or tree or a mountain off in the distance. Mostly, I didn't know the answers, but I would fake some kind of response or refer the questioner to the naturalist who was at The Fall River Visitors Center at the top of the pass. A frequent question involved the area above timberline inhabited by many marmots, fat, furry, brown creatures that lived in crevices in the rocks. Tourists would often ask me about the "woodchucks" and I would explain that they were indeed marmots, a large, indigenous, vegetarian rodent.

THE C C C CAMP

When I arrived at the Grand Lake Ranger Station in early June for my first summer of work there, I found that a Civilian Conservation Corps camp had been recently established by the U.S. Army in the Endovalley area of our district. A major and a captain in the regular army were in charge. Major Albertson was a somewhat overweight, portly little man and when in full uniform with puttees on his fat legs and wearing his wide-brimmed army hat, he still didn't look quite military.

He had a habitual expression of extreme boredom and resentment, fortunately modulated by his sardonic sense of humor at finding himself in this position in his Army career. He once said to me, "I'd never have believed that in joining the United States Army I'd be sent to a place deep in the mountains with a hundred underprivileged hoodlums to whom I had to issue condoms every Saturday night." I said that I didn't realize this was part of his job but he said, "Yeah, we really have to do that if they want them."

He did not betray these thoughts that so distressed him to just anybody, but I got to know him well enough so that he knew I would listen but would not repeat any of his confidences. The two officers were assisted by a couple of sergeants and a dozen other enlisted personnel, including two cooks. The first sergeant was a tough old combat veteran named Gene Strike. He knew that the CCC boys were not real dogface soldiers and could not be expected to be handled with military discipline. He had an organizational turn of mind and the major depended on him to carry out their mission and pretty much run the camp. The boys called him "Sarge" or "Sir" with deep respect. The ultimate disciplinary measure available was that any seriously disruptive or trouble-making boy could be sent home promptly and without a hearing.

The camp accommodated about a hundred young men, many from Denver and cities in Kansas and Oklahoma. They would arrive in buses from these cities, were from eighteen to twenty-five years old and mostly looked pale and not very happy. After a month or two in the schedule of outdoor work and all the food they could eat, their attitudes and appearance were much improved. Most of the work was rebuilding existing trails up into the mountains and making new trails into the high country above the timberline. Each morning the boys were turned out at six o'clock and given a large breakfast of eggs, pancakes, sausage, toast, coffee, and orange juice that was put out on the tables in large platters and pitchers. The workers were taken out to the various jobs at about eight o'clock, each carrying a bag lunch. They worked until noon, had a half-hour for lunch, worked again until about four P.M. then back to the camp. Five thirty was dinner time when they were given a huge meal of meat, potatoes, vegetables, fruit, and apple pie.

After a couple of months of this kind of life, they were tanned and healthy and appeared to be reasonably happy about the whole situation. They were paid a dollar a day, they could leave the camp for an evening if given a ride and had to be back in camp by 11 P.M. Many stayed in camp and played cards.

Those of us in the Park Service called them "Woodpeckers" and the CCC Camp was the "Woodpecker Camp." They were looked upon as being somewhat socially suspect and the many available young ladies, tourists, or those working in the resorts didn't quite know how to deal with the CCC boys.

I came to know the two officers quite well and I made it a point to listen to their complaints about being "in this god-forsaken place." I tried to be sympathetic to their concerns, but I did not share their negative feelings about running the CCC Camp. I was having the time of my life at age twenty and of course, had an entirely different attitude about my lifestyle as a temporary ranger. The work of the camp was supervised by daytime employees of the Park Service, the Forestry Service, and sometimes by the Bureau of Public Roads. The latter planned a program cooperating with the Park Service and the CCC Camp to clean up the trash that accumulated every few days along the highway from the Grand Lake Entrance to the Fall River Pass, a distance of about thirty-five miles. Once a week, I would take two boys from the CCC Camp and drive slowly up the road through the park with a boy sitting on each front fender of my Chevy patrol truck. The trash to be found on the shoulder of the highway and in the paralleling ditches was mostly candy and gum wrappers, beer and soda cans, bottles of many descriptions, and other paper and metal throwaways. The fenders on my 1930 Chevy pickup were generous enough so that a boy could sit on each one, leaning on the hood and be reasonably safe and comfortable. I would drive at about ten miles an hour and as a boy saw a piece of trash, he would raise his arm and I would stop and he would dash over to pick it up, throw it into a bin in the back of the truck, and jump back to his seat on the front fender. This was a system invented by the first two boys who were given this job by the first sergeant. At first they had ridden in the back of the truck, but it was awkward scrambling in and out so we all agreed to try the front fender system. This assignment was considered to be a desirable day's work because we would start at eight o'clock and finish at about three in the afternoon. It was much less strenuous than wielding a shovel, an axe or a machete all day building or repairing trails. We got to be quite chummy on these weekly trash pick-up days. The boys told me much about their families, their schools, and their hopes and ambitions. Most of them came from families or situations of reduced financial circumstances as the country was still in the depths of the Depression and the hard times felt by almost everybody. The boys knew that the work would stop in the early fall and the CCC Camp would close when the snow fell and the highway through the park would be closed for the winter. I told them my job would stop in late September and I was going back to school in Chicago. At the end of each day of trash pick-up, I would deliver the boys back to the camp and sometimes stay until 5:30 in the afternoon to have dinner with the officers at their table in the dining room. For this, I was charged a dollar and a half.

Among the civilians hired by each CCC Camp at that time was an "Education Director," whose job was very loosely defined. He was in charge of a very modest library set up in one of the large tents with a few shelves of books and a few tables with straight chairs, not very comfortable or conducive to deep thoughts. The education director was Joe Chay, from San Francisco. He was a graduate student at the University of California at Berkeley where he had been an undergraduate and was now on the way to getting a master's degree in English literature. He was also a practical man who made himself at home in the camp as best he could. He lived in the officer's quarters with them on a fairly pleasant basis, but he was never close to them. They didn't like what they were doing. Joe Chay took a much more light-hearted, occasionally cynical approach to his work and tried to organize a few activities that could be voluntarily attended by the boys. I happened to mention to him that I had recently completed a course at the university in *The Great War And The New Europe*, given by Frederick L. Schuman, and including what happened from 1914 to 1933 and the beginning of the Nazi dictatorship. World War II was still four years away. I had my notes on the course in my book bag and Joe and I had vigorous discussions about the state of the world after World War I. After one of these conversations, Joe said," Why don't you come over here at about seven o'clock one evening and talk to some of the boys about this. Don't come in your ranger uniform. Come in street clothes and carry some books."

He was able to attract about a dozen boys who came into the library tent where a few folding wooden chairs had been set up and a card table for me in front. Joe instructed me, "Give them a run-down on the World War, the peace treaty, and the League of Nations. See if you can get any of these kids to ask you some questions." I viewed this whole exercise as a small favor to my new friend Joe Chay and I gave it the best I could. I made a narrative of the events leading to Wilson's failure to get the Senate to approve and so have the United States join the proposed League of Nations and the long-term negative consequences.

When my 15-minute presentation over, the few questions they asked had nothing to do with the subject of my amateur lecture. I had been introduced to the boys beforehand by Joe as "My friend, Sam Hair." When I finished talking, no one said anything for a minute or two, then one of the boys raised his hand and said, "Hey, Sam, you're a ranger aren't you?"

"Well, yes. That's my job here in the park."

"How do you get a job like that?"

"Well, I have a temporary summer job. To get a full time ranger job, you have to go to forestry school." I wanted to get away from this line of questions as quickly as possible, so when the boy persisted and said, "How do I get a temporary summer job like yours?" Joe stood up and said, "Fellas, it's a busy day tomorrow. Thanks, Sam, for telling us about this important part of our recent history. All right boys, we can adjourn now. Good night everybody."

I did not make any further attempts to elevate the intellectual interests of the CCC boys, but Joe and I were frequently together after hours discussing the peculiar ways of the park service world as well as those of the United States Army and the Civilian Conservation Corps. If Joe was so inclined, he could and did recite much of T. S. Elliott including, to my enjoyment, some of the poetic adventures of cats and "The Love Song of J. Alfred Prufrock." To hear this on a quiet evening in a place where nobody read anything except occasionally the *Denver Post* was refreshing to me. I was impressed with Joe's erudition, we enjoyed each other's company, and we needed each other for any kind of stimulating conversation.

Once a week or so we would go to the Phantom Valley Ranch for dinner, a privately owned upscale dude outfit inside the park. We were encouraged to do this by Lynn Gilham, the owner, who liked to have us there to mingle with the guests and have a couple of drinks. These were jolly occasions, with liquor flowing freely, followed by a bountiful dinner.

One of the guests was a second generation member of a prominent hotel family. His name was Ellsworth and he was there at the ranch alone with his Mercer Runabout, a rare collector's car even then. He was a small dark-haired man; his hard-looking, thin, pinched face made him look older than his thirty-something years. He was between wives of which he had had two. He had his own horse at the ranch and when he wasn't out with his Mercer, he was on his horse riding the many trails up into the Never Summer Range.

Sometimes on my highway patrol duty I would have to turn on my siren and have Ellsworth pull over, stopped for driving sixty miles and hour in the thirty-five mile zone. He would always say he didn't know he was going that fast and I would always believe him, tell him to be careful, and let him go. We both knew that if I ever arrested him and took him over to Estes Park to the United States Commissioner, they would fine him $50.00 for speeding. It could take up to an entire day for both of us to do it and Lynn Gilham would never again have me as his guest for dinner at the ranch. So, Ellsworth drove pretty much as he wanted to, but had sense enough to be generally careful and not too wildly reckless.

1935–Sam Hair, Park Ranger

CHARLEY HALLENBECK

Another man whom I could not and did not ever pull over for speeding was Charley Hallenbeck, the general contractor for the paving of the recently completed last eleven miles of the new Trail Ridge Road. This was then, and may still be, the highest federal highway in our country, maybe in the world, at something over 12,000 feet at the top of the pass coming from Estes Park to Grand Lake, the west and east entrances to Rocky Mountain Park. In my daily journeys to the end of our district at the pass, the work on several miles of paving above the timberline was progressing slowly. One lane of traffic going in one direction was kept open so that a pickup truck with a red flag could escort a group of cars to one end of the paving work and escort another group going back in the other direction. The work of building the road was completed and ready to be paved, but there were occasional rock falls onto the area to be paved. This enraged Charley Hallenbeck because he was going to be charged a penalty for every day of non-completion beyond his contractual completion date.

In the 1930s, the work of asphalt paving in the high country was not easily done. At the beginning of the work in early June, Charley had a brand new, top-of-the-line Buick Roadmaster four-door sedan as his personal vehicle which he used to drive from one end of the job to the other as fast as he could go. After a few weeks of his driving his new car, formerly a tan color, was now mostly black with large patches of solidified asphalt all over it. He would exhort his crews to speed up the work and he brought in a grader hired from another contractor in Granby to clear various clumps of large rocks that had fallen into the areas ready to be paved. I sometimes stopped where I could do so without getting in the way, and if he was anywhere nearby I would try to engage him in a conversation. Usually, he didn't want to talk to me because he had learned to be suspicious of anyone in uniform, but he was finally convinced I was only watching and not monitoring anything. He eventually talked rather freely, revealing himself to be a frustrated human being dealing with a Sisyphean task every day and cursing rock slides with a stream of creative profanity.

"Those insignificant little sons of bitches at the BPR," he would mutter with undisguised contempt. "They're no goddamn help to me. When I tell them about the rock slides, they say, 'You deal with it, Charley.'" The work was finished by the end of the summer with traffic flowing freely between the eastern and western park entrances. I did not hear that Charley Hallenbeck suffered any penalties for a late completion of the paving. I was then and always have been impressed with his hard-driving persistence that got the job done while overcoming what appeared to be insurmountable obstacles created by man and nature.

A DINNER IN THE NEVER SUMMER

My second summer of work at Rocky Mountain Park was my first at the Grand Lake Ranger Station where Fred McLaren was district ranger. When we learned of our assignments in early June in Estes Park, I was happy to be told I was to report to Fred. I went over the pass with my heavy suitcase in one of the old red buses authorized to carry passengers between Estes Park and Grand Lake, the east and west park entrances. The buses were owned by a Denver man named Rowe Emory. In earlier years transportation between the east and west park had been Stanley Steamers, well-suited for heavy-duty mountain travel, but those vehicles now were no longer manufactured or used. The succeeding gasoline-powered buses were already somewhat antiquated and required many shift-downs to get up the mountain at about twenty mph and down as fast as the driver wanted to go without panicking the passengers.

The driver dropped me off at the Grand Lake Entrance, which was also where I was to live. There were four of us in that cabin: John Meston, Ernie Fields, Sterling Vaughn, and me. Right away, Fred put us to work repairing our living quarters that, among other things, needed a new floor. Having never driven a nail in my whole life, I sat around and watched Sterling do most of the work, helped somewhat by John and Ernie. This was my first acquaintance with Sterling and he became a lifelong friend whom I admired then and still do after more than sixty years.

I never knew anybody who could do carpentry, build fences, ride horses, wrangle horses, take care of horses, (yes) shoe horses and who could do anything Fred said to do. Also, we shared very deep philosophical discussions about important subjects like women and where we were going that night. Everybody in Grand Lake knew Sterling, including the waitresses at the Pine Cone Inn and all those at Humphrey's Store, Bill's Cafe, and the Grand Lake Drugstore.

There was also the staff at the Grand Lake Lodge who knew Sterling and where we could get a full-course dinner for fifty cents. One evening early in the summer we went up to the Lodge for dinner and were told that we were no longer allowed to eat in the main dining room and we would have to eat with the employees in a small place off the kitchen. Sterling and I decided this was an unthinkable affront to our dignity and we decided never to darken the doorstep of the Grand Lake Lodge again. A few days later, we were told that all was forgiven and would we please come back and eat in the main dining room with the guests as we always had. It seems that rangers in uniform were good to have around just for visibility. It also gave us a chance to get acquainted with all the young lady school teachers on vacation and guests at the Lodge who should have been terrified of us but were not.

My job that summer was highway patrol and I was given a Ford V-8 pickup truck, suitable for that and other miscellaneous duties, with a large, shiny siren. I was to cover the highway within the park from Grand Lake to the Fall River Pass, a distance of about thirty five miles.

Sterling's job was horseback trail patrol up into the high country in two directions to the north and east, each on alternating days. He was also to take care of several Park Service horses at the McLaren corral where Fred and his family lived. Our activities seemed to include long days of work at the height of the tourist season and equally long nights at The Pine Cone Inn in town.

The following summer, Sterling was sent up to an outpost patrol job in the Never Summer Range in the northwest portion of the park composed of several peaks exceeding 12,500 feet. His camp was at about the timberline at 10,000 feet near Thunder Pass, which was 11,300 feet. He was the only one who could do this as the job required someone who could live up there in a one-room cabin with a saddle horse, two pack horses, and live on groceries brought in to him. It was a difficult and lonesome proposition.

Every week I had a day off. One afternoon after work I drove to Phantom Valley Ranch, the location of the trail-head up into the Never Summer. Lynn Gilham, the ranch manager, as always, gave me a horse to ride up into the Never Summer carrying two large saddle-bags filled with much-needed groceries for Sterling.

This involved finding his camp, which I thought I never would after the first two hours. I had to go up through Lulu City, an abandoned mining town, and then take a trail I wasn't sure of. I had never been to Sterling's camp before and I was following Fred McLaren's instructions. It was further than I realized and soon I thought I must be lost. It was also getting dark, but my horse seemed to know we were heading toward other horses, so we went along at a fast walk. Shortly after dark I saw a light ahead which was like a beacon to a storm-tossed mariner for I knew it had to be Sterling's camp, way up in the Never Summer in the middle of nowhere.

With great good cheer, and to my immense relief, Sterling came out and brought in my saddle bags and put away my horse. We settled down in the warm cabin, out of the cold, with a quart of Canadian whiskey in the light of a Coleman gas lantern. Sterling had had enough time alone in the wilderness to learn the fundamentals of preparing a meal and he outdid himself as he always did for anyone bringing him supplies from Grand Lake. He fixed large steaks, country fried potatoes, lima beans and he opened a ready-made chocolate cake. We talked of the Park Service, women, and the many variables in the lives of young men that we could neither understand nor do anything about. After the long day and my long ride, we went to bed early and slept late.

The next day was my day off so I rode back down to Phantom Valley and got there about noon in time for lunch. But if anybody ever asks me what was the best meal I ever had, I would say without hesitation it was the steak dinner at the end of a long day in the mountains of Colorado when I was ravenously hungry–that dinner fixed by Sterling Vaughn.

In later years, Sterling raised a great and happy family and enriched the lives of his friends. On his birthday I wrote him, "Dear Sterling: The gods may be laughing at us, but we've had a good ride. Here's to your happy 90th, and may you have many more . . ."

1936–Sterling Vaughn

PETE SZYMANSKI

The end of September was the end of my first summer of work on the Grand Lake side of Rocky Mountain Park under the tutelage of Fred McLaren. There was a diminished number of tourists and not much to do. The CCC Camp was closed down at the end of August, the boys evacuated, the army personnel all reassigned, and the civilian employees left to their own devices. Joe Chay went back to San Francisco and to more study at Berkeley. The tents at the camp, with their wood-floor frames, were taken down and removed. Only the four permanent buildings were left to a caretaker who lived in one of them. The camp was enclosed by a fence, wire with 4x4 hardwood posts sunk in concrete with a large gate at the entrance always open in the summer but now closed and locked. The caretaker was to keep the area clear of overgrown shrubbery, protect the buildings from unlawful occupants, and generally to keep the camp in condition for reopening the following June. The caretaker was Pete Syzmanski and his wife Bruhl. In my highway patrol job I had to drive by the camp nearly every day and when everybody was gone, I stopped at the gate and saw Pete for the first time. He was working nearby and came over to the gate to let me in. He was a spare, bespectacled, soft-spoken man in his early thirties who always appeared to be cheerful. When in conversation, he came across as one not only highly-educated but one who spoke as if any subject worth discussing was worth discussing analytically and arriving at some conclusion about it—all very non-confrontational and all very respectful of the other person's judgments.

As a ranger in uniform, I had every right to inspect his premises and he walked around with me to see a large part of the now abandoned camp area. He invited me into one of the four frame buildings which the army had converted into living quarters for him. These were the former officers' quarters and administrative offices, one of which had been up fitted with a kitchen and partitioned into a living room, two bedrooms, and a bath. Pete had fixed up the living room into a sort of library-sitting-room with one wall covered with bookcases, a wood-burning stove, a sofa with two large end tables, a couple of armchairs, and new carpet throughout.

We sat for a few minutes and chatted about the closing of the CCC Camp and I couldn't help but notice some of the books in a four-shelf bookcase against the opposite wall. One in particular was *The Count of Monte Cristo*, which I took from the shelf and opened to find it was in French. There were others including *Anna Karenina* in Russian, *The Odyssey* in Greek and Caesar's

Gallic Wars in Latin. Still others were in English, including St. Augustine's *The City of God* and George Santayana's *The Realm of Essence.*

I said to Pete, "You have a wide selection here."

"Enough to keep me amused, but not enough to keep me interested."

"Do you read all these? The Greek, the French, the Russian?"

He dismissed the question, saying, "Oh, yes," as if to say, "doesn't everybody?"

A few more questions gained from him that he had been a language teacher in a Philadelphia high school until he decided to come to the high country for his health. He had a master's degree from Harvard in Slavic languages, but was also fluent in French and Greek and had taught Latin. He said he didn't mind being the caretaker of a CCC Camp in the high mountains because he had been told by his doctors that the Colorado climate would be beneficial. Also, the job gave him all the time he needed to catch up on his reading. He had a card for the public library in Estes Park where he said he could find a pretty good selection of reference works and some classics in religion and philosophy. So, there he was for the winter.

At the end of September when my job ended, I had two days before I had to leave for home. I was free to stay in the ranger-station and I had the use of a pickup truck for any errands. October 1 was the beginning of deer season and Pete asked me if I wanted to go hunting in the Arapahoe Forest outside the Park. I said I would, but I didn't have a gun and didn't know anything about hunting deer or any other animal. He said, "Well, all right, but come with me and we'll go out tomorrow for awhile."

Early the next morning, he picked me up and we went for breakfast in Grand Lake. We then took the highway south about halfway to Granby outside the Park then turned off on a side road that took us deep into a dense and deserted part of the national forest. We parked the truck and Pete handed me a monstrous Winchester lever-action 45-70, fully loaded and suitable for bringing down grizzly bears or elephants.

He said, rather apologetically, "This is the only other gun I could find, but it will do for today." Pete carried a traditional deer rifle, the Winchester model 94, lever action carbine 30-30, a favorite in the west for many years.

We never saw a deer that day. After about two hours of walking slowly through the woods, I was pretty sure we were not going to shoot at anything and we didn't. Mostly, we talked about the world political and economic situation and what could be done about the Great Depression and how fortunate we were to have jobs that paid us for doing something we found to be reasonably enjoyable. We wandered slowly back to the truck and Pete drove us back to where I was staying at the ranger station.

Probably Pete had no intention of getting me into a serious deer hunt. He had a fondness for wandering through the woods, a la Thoreau, and indulging in solemn conversation with someone he thought might take an active part. I found out enough about him in this and subsequent conversations to learn that his wife Bruhl had been a grade-school teacher in Philadelphia, that they had no children and no immediate relatives. Pete had applied for a teaching job in a high school in Granby, a nearby town west of the park, beginning in the fall of the following year. He said he didn't mind looking after an abandoned CCC Camp for one winter, but Bruhl thought he should not make a career of it.

This began a friendship that continued through the remaining summers of my job at the national park. Pete was teaching at a high school in Salida, Colorado for several years, during which time we developed a regular correspondence. His letters came frequently and were models of erudite and amusing composition. I told him in April of 1937 of my final appointment to the ranger job and that I was to take the train to Denver from Chicago in early June, the bus from Denver to Grand Lake and report for duty June 7. He telephoned me shortly thereafter and said he was driving to Philadelphia for some business reasons and that he could arrange to drive back from there to Chicago, pick me up on June 3 and we could drive together to Colorado and Grand Lake. "Good!" I told him, "Yes, we'll do it."

This turned out to be a trip that was more of an adventure that I expected because Pete cared nothing about such small comforts as hotel rooms or even motor courts. He was driving a two-door Chevrolet sedan that was about five years old. The trunk and back seat were loaded with his bags, a few possessions retrieved from his trip to Philadelphia, and my large duffel bag and canvas book bag. There were no motels as we know them now. The first day out of Chicago we drove about 350 miles and slept in a public campground on the outskirts of Des Moines, outdoors and in sleeping bags. We ate only in roadside restaurants and did not have a bath or shave the entire trip. Pete handled this better than I did.

The second day we drove to North Platte and another public campground and another night in our sleeping bags. So far, we had been on US Highway 30, "The Lincoln Highway." The third day, west of North Platte, we turned south on Highway 6 to Denver and Highway 108 north to Estes Park, arriving there just before dark. Pete dropped me off at the Hupp Hotel where I could get a room, get cleaned up and have the luxury of a large dinner served on a table with a white table cloth.

In spite of the rough and ready manner in which we made this trip, Pete was always cheerful and given to quoting Latin aphorisms, or obscure foreign words and phrases when the going became uncomfortable. He had made his life into that of an outdoorsman, possibly even approving of some discomforts as a form of discipline. My lifestyle was not yet that fully developed. If I was taken away from the usual pattern of bathing, shaving, and changing underwear every day, I did not need my mother to tell me I was dirty and smelled bad. But, it was a happy trip and I paid for only half the gas and oil and my meals in the restaurants or a total of less than $40.00. The trip also probably became the basis of a lifelong friendship with Pete Syzmanski, even though in later years we went in different directions.

Pete stayed in the west and I remained in Chicago until the spring of 1942 when I reported to the Glenview Naval Air Station, north of the city, for aviation training. In August, I went to NAS Jacksonville, Florida to complete the V-5 Aviation Cadet program. I was commissioned and given my wings in January, 1943, a very large event in my life.

My correspondence with Pete continued, with interruptions, for the next forty years. I saved his letters because he always gave his analytical mind full rein, even on trivial matters. (Pete had earlier explained to me that the word "trivial" came from the Latin "tri via," or a place where three roads came together and travelers would meet and discuss news and gossip.)

A letter addressed to me at the Fleet P.O. in New York reported that he had revisited Rocky Mountain National Park and that Grand Lake was a "ghost town" with most stores and all hotels and guest ranches closed. He had volunteered to work during the summer at the Denver ordnance plant until his teaching job started in Salida. The Denver job was a difficult one with long hours and frequent weekend work. At the Salida High School he would teach three classes in world history.

A letter from Salida in June, 1947 said he had received an offer from Western State College in Gunnison, Colorado to teach two classes in Russian and one in sociology beginning the following September.

He wrote to me from the college in Gunnison in June, 1949 in response to my letter of telling him of my departure from the ranks of bachelordom at the advanced age of 34:

My Dear Sam,

This should be another apologia pro vita sua, but since I know I should fail in the attempt, I shall limit it to a few faltering remarks and rest upon your mercy for clemency. I seem to have needed time to catch my breath with which to wish you and Mrs. Hair MANY HAPPY YEARS TOGETHER. I had hoped–a hope slowly vanishing–that you might find your way hither and that Bruhl and I should have the opportunity of expressing this wish more directly. But I am afraid that only this stilted manner is left to us to say what we deeply feel.

Do take this as a patriarchal blessing to both of you. Teach me to know you in the plural, as I knew you once in the singular. Write to me more often. And when the spirit moves you, may He deign to send you both our way.

Love and regards,
Pete

Eight years later, we again exchanged letters. His in reply to mine came in July, 1958:

Bruhl and I continue to enjoy life in our own peculiar way. I came here to Western State as a professor of history and have lately succeeded to the chairmanship of the social studies division. My salary I accept not without some sense of guilt, but give no vocal expression to that feeling. We have a rather large home on four acres, one mile out of Gunnison, and at times, especially while resting and reading in our sun-room, I fancy myself a country gentleman.

There followed a regrettable interval when I neglected to keep our correspondence going until 1977. I phoned the college and they gave me his address in Eugene, Oregon, where he had removed since retiring from there in 1962 at the age of 65. We began another series of exchanges of letters for six years, the last coming from Pete in March, 1983.

In May 1984, a letter came from Bruhl containing news which I somehow suspected would come because they had not acknowledged my Christmas letter the previous December.

Some letters are easy to write–this one isn't. Pete died peacefully in his sleep April 19. He had a recent series of small strokes and a bad fall which caused a hip fracture. He lived for three months after the hip surgery. Our partnership lasted for 54 years. He valued his memories of you, Sam . . . Pete and I send you our love and our hope that life will be good to you and your family.

Bruhl

A few months later, she wrote again:

Dear Sam,
I found something Pete wrote on the occasion of his retirement from Western State in 1962 when the staff gave a party for him. . . . It reminded me of Pete's wonderful sense of humor and I thought you would enjoy it, too.

Love,
Bruhl

A MATTER OF SCANT INTEREST
Western's campus adequately shows
That fashion is no slave to reason:
That daring girls now shed their clothes,
Since lack of clothes is chic this season.

Gone are the days of obfuscation:
That sheath, that wasping of the waist,
That tendency toward hip inflation . . .
Depressing then avoided haste.

The ladies who proclaimed the mode
Which ruffled up the derriere
Were probably the ones who showed
Unnatural protrusion there.

The waistline dropped around the thighs
Was certainly the very canny
Invention of a girl whose prize
Was rather a restricted fanny.

The fulsome horizontal bulge,
The bust of hyperdensity,
Was surely fashioned to indulge
A natural propensity.

Then ladies who had knees that touch,
and those with knees somewhat akimbo
Were not complaining over much
Since style consigned their limbs to limbo.

'Twas obvious then that all that clatter
For pinching here, and plumping there,
Reduced it all to the awkward matter
Of who had what, and had it where.

The women since have called a stop,
And cast a glove in fashion's teeth,
Now dress with little on the top,
And almost nothing underneath.

When all my days are ending,
And I have no song to sing,
I think I shall not be too old
To look and stare at everything
As I once stared at a nursery door,
Or a tall tree, and a swing.

Pete Szymanski
June 1962, Western State College, Colorado

I was glad to receive Pete's cheerful observation in poetic form of the changes in feminine fashion. I noted the last six lines were a sort of elegy added to the longer verse, perhaps his way of expressing a farewell gesture to his friends. Pete was an iconoclast, an intellectual adventurer, and a loyal and devoted friend. I was my privilege to know him and to be touched by him for a large part of both our lives.

1935–Pete and Bruhl Szymanski

IV. THE UNIVERSITY

PHIL ALLEN

My final quarter at the University of Chicago was one that I enjoyed more than any other because I had satisfied all the requirements for graduation except for a few electives of my own choosing. One of these was "Masterpieces of Greece and Rome" and Thornton Wilder was the instructor. He had been a classmate at Yale of our university president, Robert M. Hutchins, and Henry Luce, The *Time Magazine* founder. Hutchins brought Wilder to the university to teach two classes in the Greek classics for which there was great demand and a long waiting list to be included in each class of forty, a limit established by Wilder. He had recently written a highly successful novel, *The Bridge of San Luis Rey*, and was a genuine literary celebrity. He was well-grounded in this field of classical drama and easily approachable by any of us who wanted to talk to him.

Another elective that I chose was "The German Novella From Goethe to Thomas Mann," a seminar that met once a week on Wednesday for two hours. Philip Schuyler Allen, a full professor and head of the German Department, was the instructor. There were only six in this seminar and we met in a small classroom in Harper Library near Dr. Allen's office, deep in the library stacks. There were no prerequisites for the course, no German language required and all we had to do was read five German novellas (translated into English). We would meet in the small classroom and Dr. Allen would be sitting in an armchair at the front of the room. He never brought in any notes or books. He just talked in a sort of random way about this particular aspect of German fiction and invited opinions and discussion.

He was one of the older department heads and was graduated from Williams College in 1891. He spent two years at the University of Berlin and then received his Ph.D in German literature at the University of Chicago in 1897. He was a member of one of the early football teams coached by Amos Alonzo Stagg, who put the team into the Big Ten Conference when it was formed. He was known as Phil Allen, always spoken as if it were one word. He was a repository of stories about the early days of the university, which he described as "the greatest collection of scholars in one place since fifth century Athens." He had written half a dozen books for publishers of introductory texts for the teaching of German, French, and Latin languages in high schools. He refereed Big Ten football games for fifteen years after his playing days, when those officials were underpaid amateurs who did it for expense money on Saturdays.

He had known my father, who was a graduate of the class of 1903, and so when I appeared as a member of the class for the study of the German novella, he knew something about me and was cordial and forthcoming from the beginning of our acquaintance. During the month of April, we met in the Harper Library classroom and by the end of the month, the six of us in the class had become quite chummy and enjoyed being together. What we did know, but soon found out, was that every day at 5:30 P.M., Phil Allen could be found at the University Grill, a tavern on 55th Street at Woodlawn Avenue. After about a month of our seminar discussions, he suggested that any of us who felt so inclined could walk with him the four blocks to 55th Street and have a drink before going home. Some of us took him up on it because it was one situation where he could and would discuss the early days of the university and some of his football experiences. After a few of these get-togethers at the University Grill, Professor Allen began to think it was a good idea to begin the seminar there at three o'clock each Wednesday as it appeared that most of us were going there anyway a little later in the afternoon. There were two students in the seminar who had not been going with him to the tavern on 55th Street, but they said they didn't mind going there to discuss German literature, so it was arranged that we would meet at the University Grill for the remaining Wednesday seminars. At that final meeting of the group, we had to spend the two hours in the classroom writing essay answers to about a dozen questions about the five novellas being considered in the course. The questions were asked in such a way that almost any answer indicated that you had indeed read those books. We found out later that all of us got "Bs." At that time, there was not much hustling for "As" in these elective courses and everyone was satisfied with the "B."

Before going any further in my recollection of the last part of Phil Allen's life, I must say that no part of it is meant to demean him or his behavior at the time. He never lost his dignity or his essential courtesy to others, nor did he lose the respect of his confreres on the faculty. He enjoyed recounting some of the episodes of his time in the early university setting, some of which were ribald, some very sad. One of the latter was about his friend and colleague Robert Morss Lovett, a professor of English and an editor of *The Nation*. Dr. Lovett's only son, "Bimbles," was killed in France in the First World War and the news came to him as he was on his way to his class in Elizabethan drama. He read the telegram and proceeded on his way to the class, gave his full attention to his lecture and was then notified to go to the home of Dr. Burton, the then president of the university, where a group of his friends had assembled. A few days later, he took leave to go to France to bring home the body of his son.

I became more than a student in Phil Allen's class and found the time to be with him for an hour or so at the University Grill in the late afternoon a couple of days each week. During our two-hour seminars in the back of the tavern, at a large table which was set aside for us, he would have two or three tall highballs of Old McBrayer Scotch, which they kept there for him. Other days, he would be there from five o'clock until at least seven when he would walk the two blocks to his apartment at 58th & Drexel Avenue. I did not know then, and could see it only later, that he was trying to destroy himself, but maybe he didn't know it. During my time at the university, he remained as head of the German Department, but his office staff and instructors and assistant professors did the necessary teaching and administrative work. He was accepted by the university administration as a competent department head and one of their senior scholars. By his associates, who were full professors, and his peers, he was seen to be a man whose achievements were great, but were in the past and behind him. They all thought he drank too much, but never told him so. He had close, devoted friends including Ferdinand Schevill, John Nef, Robert Morss Lovett, and Albion Small, all eminent faculty members. When with them, he was all good humor and being a jocular good fellow came easily. Some of these friends, including Phil Allen, had summer places at Lake Zurich, a suburb to the north and west of Chicago. They spent most of the summer there and their children grew up together out there.

In addition to his books on language instruction, he had written two definitive books on medieval poetry: *The Romanesque Lyric* and *The Medieval Latin Lyric* which were enough to put him into the realm of leading medievalists. He was also the founder and one of the editors of *National Philology*, a quarterly periodical. I learned that he had at one time written an article on Mariolotry for the *Americana Encyclopaedia*.

I found out in conversations with him that he lived alone, that his wife Jess had died two years ago and that he had a housekeeper who came in every day for two hours and cleaned up the apartment and did his laundry. I could not figure out where he got his meals, but I heard that he went to the Quadrangle Club for breakfast, didn't eat any lunch, and put together some kind of an evening meal for himself at the apartment. Betty Ito, a Japanese student working on a master's degree in medieval history and in our seminar, told me this about his meals.

She said to me one afternoon at the University Grill when the seminar was over, "I've told Professor Allen I was coming over to his apartment at seven o'clock and fix dinner for him. Would you like to come and help me?" I thought this was a great idea and said, yes, I'd be there. I walked with the professor from the University Grill to his apartment at about six-thirty and Betty Ito came shortly thereafter with two large bags containing all the wherewithal for a dinner of small steaks, fried potatoes, and string beans, which she fixed in the kitchen while the professor and I were in the front room. He had another Old McBrayer highball, and it loosened him up to one of his narrative moods about the old University. He had an impressively large capacity to drink Scotch for several hours and not be more than a little garrulous and never slurring his words. Betty Ito was a porcelain-doll type of classic oriental beauty from a prominent family in California and kept most of the college boys at a distance. She was seen mostly with female companions. She enjoyed vigorous discussions with Professor Allen about Latin literature and he engaged in friendly arguments with her about the fine points of medieval architecture. She did well, I learned later, and got her master's degree with honors.

After dinner, we stayed until ten o'clock. Both of us left together, she to her dormitory and I to walk down to Kimbark Avenue and home.

I saw Professor Allen frequently after that in several different places. He gave me a key to his office in Harper Library where I could study or use his telephone when he wasn't there. The office had large leaded glass windows behind his desk looking out over the Midway and bookcases from floor to ceiling on two of the walls. It was deep in the library stacks and away from the German Department offices on another floor of the library. Being in there alone and in a perfectly quiet, scholarly atmosphere, I felt that I could think deep thoughts and absorb some of the academic sanctity of the place. I also read all of Aldous Huxley beginning with *Brave New World*, which everybody was talking about then. The professor was generous with books that he no longer needed and gave me several that he was going to give to the library and that I still have today. He had an old typewriter in his office with two sets of "QWERTY" keyboards, one for capital and one for lower case letters. It was on this machine that he had, over the years, produced his books and dozens of published articles. I read some of his typescripts that he had in his files. They were typed in perfect paragraphs with no errors, ready to go to the publishers. He did, however, admit to writing everything first in longhand on a yellow pad. That was where he made any revisions. He often got a graduate student who could read his writing to help out with the typing.

After graduation, I went to New York on a Greyhound bus to look for a job anywhere I could find one, preferably on a newspaper or magazine. I had a letter from Thornton Wilder addressed to Henry Luce ("Dear Harry . . .") which he wrote for me to take to the offices of *Time Magazine* to see if I could get an appointment to see The Founder. It turned out that that Mr. Luce was in the Caribbean on a honeymoon trip with Clare Booth and I was referred to Daniel Longwell, one of the editors of *Life*. The following day I went back for two interviews with others on the staff of *Life*, after which I was told, "Don't call us. We'll call you." I had the feeling that I would never hear from them, and I never did.

It was a very easy choice for me to decide to forget about finding a journalism job in New York and to request my reappointment as a temporary ranger in Rocky Mountain National Park. My father sent another letter to Mr. Ickes and soon thereafter I received a notice from the park ordering me to be there in early June. This was the summer of 1936 and my third as a ranger.

The park closed for the season when the Fall River Pass was snowed in and in October I went back to the university to take a few post-graduate courses in history and political science. My time with the professor was somewhat diminished as I was involved in rewriting a Blackfriars musical play and editing a summary of the school year for the Cap & Gown yearbook. I could and did use the professor's office more often as he seemed to spend less time there. Mostly, he seemed to use it for his work as editor of *Modern Philology*. Betty Ito was helping him with another book, a short memoir to be called *Scintilla*, about his younger days as a student in Germany. I continued to try to see him once or twice a week in the late afternoon at the University Grill. In April I stopped in there to see if the professor was there, but he wasn't and I talked to Ted, the owner, and Lee, the bartender and Phil Allen's friend. When I asked about the professor, they said he hadn't been in for several days, that he was on sick leave from the university and was probably at home. I went to a pay phone and called his number, but there wasn't any answer. I called Betty Ito's number to see if she could tell me anything about the professor, but her roommate said that Betty had just left for California to interview for an instructor's job at the university at Berkeley in medieval European history. But I was more than curious about the professor and where he might be. The office of the German department at the university said that he was on a leave of absence because of illness. They gave me the number of his daughter in California. When I called the number, there was no answer.

One morning a few days later at home, the phone rang. It was Lee Cotter, the bartender. He said, "Hey, Sam, the professor died last night! I knew you would want to know." He was quite excited and his voice shook a little.

I said, "That's impossible. I've been calling around to see where he was and nobody said he was all that badly ill."

"Yeah, but his daughter called the doctor day before yesterday and he sent him over to Billings. He was starved and his liver wouldn't work. Ted here knows somebody at the hospital and that's what we heard. He died last night, we know that."

I was shocked, but I didn't know what to do. I thought I should do something so I called Ralph Nicholson, the editor of the *Daily Maroon*. He knew that

I knew Phil Allen more than casually so I said, "Ralph, Phil Allen died yesterday and if you want me to, I'll write his obituary for you for tomorrow."

"All right, but we need it by four o'clock."

I sat down and wrote about a thousand words, overly flowery as I read it today, with a lot of overblown admiration. I felt that way about him then and still do. I remember Phil Allen as being above and apart from the academic rivalries and politics of university people and being a part of the great and growing academic community of this outstanding university in Chicago. I thought it appropriate, somehow, that I should hear about Phil Allen's death from a bartender, but I mean not to describe the last part of his life in a way that demeans him. So, if he wanted to give a seminar of the German novella in a saloon, why not? I could always take my problems to him and he would almost always say, "Do the best you can. Most things you worry about will never happen." His academic achievements were great and maybe by my being with him occasionally in the later years of his life, he was a little less lonely. Anyway, he was my friend.

DR. LASSWELL AND LORD BUCKLEY

Harold D. Lasswell was one of the stars of the political science faculty at the University of Chicago, although he would never have so described himself. His work was unique in that group of eminent scholars in the field. He had a doctorate in political science and a master's degree in psychology. He wrote voluminously about psychopathology and politics and that was the title of one of his books. Because he described Abraham Lincoln as an "inhibited rage type," this gave me the vision of our martyred president wandering around the White House in the middle of the night, shaking with inhibited rage. Maybe Dr. Lasswell had that right.

He carried books and papers with him into class but seldom seemed to use them, usually speaking freely and in orderly paragraphs without notes. He had the enviable habit of experienced lecturers of telling us what he was going to say that day, getting into it in full detail and then summarizing the main points. He was good-natured and added much that was cynical and iconoclastic to the subjects.

It happened that one of my classmates at the Deke House had become socially acquainted with Dr. Lasswell after finding that the good doctor had a weakness, if only slight, for down-and-dirty burlesque shows and similar entertainment forms. I had meanwhile heard about a new act at a place called The Ball Of Fire, a small night club on North Clark Street. My friend, a student under Dr. Lasswell's tutelage for an advanced degree, had been to a couple of Wabash Avenue burlesque shows with Dr. Lasswell in tow, just the two of them.

I asked my friend, "Do you think he would like Dick Buckley at The Ball of Fire?" My friend said he didn't know, but to get the professor into a conversation about my studies then suggest very casually that I had heard about a new talented comic at a place on North Clark Street and see if he picks up on it. So, one day after a lecture, I stayed after class and asked the professor if I could see him for a few minutes. I walked with him toward his office nearby and when we got there, he invited me in. I settled into a straight chair opposite his desk and asked him a few questions about one of his books, which was only my way of getting him into a conversation.

I finally said, "Sir, I'm wondering if you have heard about the new very irreverent comic at a place on North Clark Street that my friend Charles Tyroler has told me about. He says that this man is a truly great and very brash performer." The professor quickly replied that, no, he hadn't, but if I would tell him where this place was, then he would think about going up there some time. Yes, perhaps he might. Very indefinite, but with a trace of interest that he did not want just anybody to see or know about. After all, he was a full professor. He was also a bachelor, wore three-piece suits the year 'round, lived alone in an apartment on Dorechester Avenue, was the author of several definitive books on political psychology, and beyond all reproach as to his habits and lifestyle. I detected something else that was not wholly surprising: this man really wanted to indulge in an occasional departure from professorial orthodoxy, so I'd take a chance and see if I could help him do it.

I said nothing more that day in his office, but a few days later, on a Friday at the end of his class, I again asked him if I could see him for a few minutes. "Yes, of course." he said. So, we walked together toward his office in the same building. On the way, I said, "Sir, I'm going to The Ball of Fire on North Clark Street tonight at about eight o'clock to hear Dick Buckley and I wondered if you would like to come with me. If you would like to do that, I can pick you up at your apartment and we can go together. There will be just the two of us."

He kept on walking for a minute or two then he stopped and turned to me and smiled. "All right, Hair. I'll see you at eight o'clock. Goodbye."

He walked on and I turned around to go to the Deke House to tell Tyroler about this. After dinner, I drove to Dr. Lasswell's apartment a few blocks away from where I lived. I was driving my mother's Packard car. The professor was waiting for me in the vestibule of the building and he came out when he saw me pull up in front. We didn't say much to each other on the way. I was too nervous to attempt to make much small talk with this eminent scholar.

When we got to Clark Street near North Avenue, I parked in a lot about a block from The Ball of Fire and we walked to its very unpretentious front entrance. The Ball of Fire was nothing but a store-front with a deep interior, the stage toward the back. Behind the stage was the kitchen area, but they served no meals, only beverages, soft and hard. There were small tables where no more than four could sit at each on small wire-backed ice-cream parlor chairs as close together as the management could put them. The Ball of Fire was fixed up like a third-rate night club, but the place was already almost full and the crowd was there for one reason—to see Dick Buckley. I had heard about him from two girls in the coffee shop at the university who were sometime friends I had known since high school. They knew me from way back and knew my occasional marginally acceptable interest in off-beat entertainment. They both more or less insisted that, "Hey, Sam, you have to go see Dick Buckley. You've never seen anything like him." A recommendation like that was to me compelling. In addition, my friend Charles Tyroler had told me that he thought Dr. Lasswell had a hidden part of his nature that might accept this type of bizarre, raunchy stand-up comedy as a form of legitimate personal investigation. He was right, as we found out.

The setting in The Ball of Fire was noisy with acoustics to match. Dick Buckley finally came on a little after nine in a totally incongruous full dress suit with white tie, tails, white gloves and a cape. I think he knew that this would make his scabrous routines all the more implausible. He had a microphone on a stand that he could lift off and carry with him in the course of his gyrations, accompanied by recorded music and sound from two speakers overhead in front of the audience. He had a young fellow assisting him as a sort of straight man and called him "Father" frequently and with exaggerated respect. When Buckley was on, he never paused. He was a strapping 180-pound six-footer and had a big voice with a wide range from bass to falsetto so his talent for mimicry and taking many parts in a sketch were all the more vivid. He never was still, strode all over the stage, bending over, jumping up and down and talking and singing. A frequent routine was several verses of a burlesque favorite, "Two Old Maids in a Folding Bed" ("One turned over to the other one, said"—followed by verses describing the frustrations of the old maids). Meanwhile, he could bug out his eyes fiercely at the audience and give them an outrageous storm of comic patter, raunchy but not downright dirty and no four-letter words, but a lot of sexual innuendo, much of it devastatingly funny.

Dr. Lasswell and I had a little table to ourselves with the soda-fountain chairs and the waiter came around to see what we wanted. The doctor said, "Bushmill's neat with water on the side and let me see the bottle, please." I ordered bourbon and ginger ale. The waiter nodded and went off and came back with a bottle of Bushmill's together with the shot glass and the glass of water on a tray with my drink. Dr. Lasswell said, "Leave the bottle, please," which the young man did. During the performance, which began at about nine o'clock and went on for about an hour, the professor had three nips of Bushmill's from the bottle and a couple of glasses of water that he would slowly sip with his Irish whiskey.

He was totally engrossed in the performance. Occasionally, he would turn to me and give me a smile of appreciation and he would sometimes mutter softly to himself, "Ah, yes," when Buckley had delivered a particularly good riff or completed an outrageous sketch. The professor was enjoying himself and I was grateful because I was the one who got him in here and I was hugely enjoying Buckley also. At later times, I was careful about describing my evening with Dr. Lasswell to just anyone because I felt that he trusted me to treat it as a private episode. I think he liked me because we had shared this evening at a disreputable night club on North Clark Street and our relationship during my remaining time at the university was guardedly congenial. I never attempted to go beyond the respectful relationship between student and teacher.

We left after the performance, each of us paying for our own drinks and a cover charge, and soon we were on the Outer Drive going south toward home. At about 39th Street, the professor said, "Hair, pull over if you will at the wide place under the bridge and stop so I can get out for a minute." There were frequent overhead bridges over the Outer Drive and under each was a wider area, enough to be out of the main traffic lanes. "I need to relieve myself," the professor said when we stopped. I had the same urgency, so we both got out of the car and went over to the nearest wall of the bridge and answered the call of nature. We had not done this at The Ball of Fire because we did not know where or if there was a men's room acceptably sanitary. Happily comforted, we got back into the car and I delivered the professor to his apartment. When we got there at about ten thirty, I stopped in front and turned off the engine. "I hope you liked Buckley, sir." I said, rather tentatively as the professor was getting out of the car. He turned to me, reached over and shook my hand. "Fascinating," he said, "Yes, fascinating. Thanks, Hair. Good night."

"Good night, sir." I said, and watched him as he went to the front door of his apartment and let himself in. I drove away and went on home. I felt that the professor and I were beginning to understand each other and I wanted to make him aware of my appreciation for this kind of shared experience. We both had a healthy curiosity about finding the outer margins of acceptable entertainment, even if the only place you could find it would be at The Ball of Fire. He said it was fascinating. Well, yes, that was one word for it, but I thought it was more than that. I thought it was absolutely great.

Buckley's rise in the entertainment business was quite rapid. After a few months at The Ball of Fire he went to a much larger place on the southwest side of Chicago on 63rd Street near Ashland Avenue. By then he had different routines and a different name—Lord Buckley. He would stand before his audience in a tuxedo and pith helmet with his lobster eyes and imperious waxed mustache giving him the look of an apoplectic English lord. To make his performance all the more incongruous, his monologues now were given in slum ghetto jive talk on religious themes such as "The Nazz" (Nazarene), a ten-minute version of the life of Jesus, and a hip version of the story of Jonah and the whale.

From Chicago he went to New York where he progressed to a famous performer, bringing out records on several different labels and lending his name to various rock groups. His famous "Hip Gan" was the fabled story of Mahatma Ghandi culminating in the naming of the "Gan's" most powerful revolutionary weapon, "The Spinning Wheel!" Buckley lived the life of the strenuous performer, boisterous and busy, and was dead at fifty-four in 1959. We who saw him in Chicago in the 1930s were among the first to see his indomitable gusto that brought joy and excitement to a middle-aged university professor and to me.

VOTE FRAUD 101

My adventure in the polling place of the 31st precinct of the 20th Ward in Chicago began when I was a graduate student at the university taking some advanced political science courses. I learned that the Chicago Association of Commerce was hiring poll watchers to be in certain selected precincts on election day. Preference was given to political science students to do this job; our instructors encouraged this, and it was almost a requirement that each student have this experience.

About twenty of us signed up for the job. We received notices in the mail that we had been appointed, that we would be paid $10.00 for the day's work, and that we were to attend a meeting to receive instructions and our credentials. The meeting was to be in a conference room at the Association of Commerce, and our instructions were to come from a "Mr. McQueeny." The meeting was scheduled for a week previous to election day, April 13, 1937, so, on April 6 at two in the afternoon we were all there.

Mr. McQueeny was sitting at a desk in front of the conference room, saying nothing until we all got there. He appeared to be in his mid-forties, sandy-haired, trim and fit, dressed in a well-tailored blue suit, white shirt and black shoes. He had been smoking a cigar, which was now in an ashtray on the desk. He stood in front of the desk and said, "I'm Terence McQueeny, and I'm a private detective."

He looked squarely at us, and spoke with a voice of authority. He explained that each selected polling place would have two of us as watchers to stay the entire day. One would be present while the other went to lunch around midday, and both of us must be there when the polling place closed and the votes were counted.

Mr. McQueeny spoke a little louder than he needed to, but that gave impetus to his instructions:

"You are here with credentials, and they can't throw you out or tell you you can't be there. Be polite always, don't get in anybody's way. Get the names of the judges and clerks, and the badge number of the policeman. You may be in a small polling place, so if it's a little crowded, just stand out of the way. The judges and clerks will sit on one side of a long table. They put the name and address of each voter in a book and give each a paper ballot. The voter goes to one of three or four curtained booths where he marks the ballot, folds it up and drops it into the ballot box on the table on his way out. It is a secret ballot. No voter can be assisted without a certificate from the election office saying he is illiterate, blind, or otherwise handicapped and needs help. You are to take notes—every hour write down the number of voters and how many needed assistance and for what reasons. There is a printed form that one of the judges has to fill out for each assisted voter, giving the reason and signed by the judge.

"There will be times when there are just a few voters and the judges and clerks have nothing much to do. If they want to start up a conversation, you can talk with them, but you must absolutely not get into voting procedures or the political process, such as, who is running for what office and how the election will turn out. Tell them nothing personal about yourself, except where you live and what you do. You have no opinions about anything. I repeat, no opinions about anything. You are a watcher, and that's all. If you see a violation of the voting procedure, write it down with the name of the judge or clerk involved, what time it happened, and say nothing about it. When the polling place closes, write down the total number of voters and the name and address of the last voter. Stay and watch while the ballots are counted, and the results tabulated and sent downtown to the election office. You are to receive a copy of the final vote count for each candidate. If they don't want to give it to you, don't insist on it. We mostly want to know about violations, if there are any. Finally, you will be with these judges and clerks for a long day. Try to be pleasant, don't get in the way. You are to complete your written report the day after the election day, deliver it here to the Association of Commerce, and you will be paid. If you have any questions, now's the time for them, and I'll answer all I can."

THE DAY BEGINS

So, armed with my credentials, on Tuesday morning, April 14, 1936, I drove to my assigned polling place at 716 DeKoven Street, a street noteworthy in Chicago history. The great Chicago Fire of 1871 allegedly started in a barn behind a house on DeKoven Street where Mrs. O'Leary's cow kicked over a lantern, setting fire to a pile of straw. Now, the Irish had long since moved elsewhere, and DeKoven Street was now part of Chicago's Italian community, as indicated by almost every name in the precinct's list of registered voters.

I arrived a little before six A.M., and parked up the street, well away from the polling place. This part of the street was then a neighborhood shopping area of small retail stores, with the polling place in one of them. The larger front part contained all the paraphernalia required to conduct the voting: the long table with chairs for the judges and clerks, the ballot box at one end, and three curtained voting booths where voters would mark their ballots. A double-door was open to a back room where there was a large table with a few straight chairs, a refrigerator, some shelving on one wall and a bathroom.

I found that my companion watcher was Larry Grandahl, whom I had met at the meeting with McQueeny, and who was also a student in political science at the university. He was a slightly built, bespectacled fellow, friendly to me and easy to be with. He did not really share my emotional involvement in a job like this, where I was determined to follow McQueeny's instructions to the letter and report back in detail any observed departures from the rectitude of the voting process.

I suppose this was because my father had served two terms as a Republican representative in the Illinois legislature in the 1920s. He had no driving political ambition, so he didn't seek a third term, but remained a Republican and a Presbyterian, in that order. His mother, my grandmother, was the daughter of Thomas J. Turner, a lawyer from Freeport, Illinois, a Whig politician and personal friend of Abraham Lincoln. They both became early Republicans, as did many Whigs, and both served one term in the United States Congress together in 1846. Turner went on to become speaker of the house in the Illinois Legislature. He corresponded with Lincoln in 1849-1850; they exchanged letters relating to their legal cases. Some of the letters from Lincoln to Turner survived and I gave them to the Illinois Historical Society collection. At the Lincoln-Douglas debate at Freeport, Illinois, in 1858 Turner was on the platform with

Lincoln and introduced him. This was my political background, clearly on the Republican side, perhaps leading me into political science study in the first place. Probably it also convinced me that the voting process was a cornerstone of American democracy, not to be tampered with by the Democratic machine in Chicago, which was then, as now, alive and well. Turner, my great grandfather, would be proud of me.

~

Those in polling place were determined to carry out the election tasks with great good will, and, later in the day, a convivial atmosphere. The judges and clerks greeted most voters by name and engaged in brief conversations while leading each to a voting booth. Frequently, a judge or a clerk would draw back the curtain, go into the booth with the voter, and assist in marking the ballot. This appeared to be not only acceptable, but a customary procedure.

By this time, I had the names of the five judges and clerks:

Republican judges:
  Fred Saviano
  Mike Corso

Democratic judge:
  Carmen Bagnola

Republican clerk:
  Alex J. Morelli

Democratic clerk:
  John Cantore

The policeman gave me his name—James O'Connell. He was a ruddy, overweight Irishman, reluctantly doing his duty by being there all day. I could read his badge number, so I didn't ask him for it. He stood, or sat, near the door until he was picked up at five o'clock when the polls closed. He took no notice of what went on in the back room later in the day, appearing to be overcome with boredom. He was there to prevent bloodshed, but "the fix was in" for him to overlook anything else.

Regarding my report, I'm sure I was including more detail in it than was Larry Grandahl in his, as he appeared to be without much comment. I was later told that his report was acceptable for its basic information, but he did not add much to that. He was never asked, as I was, to appear as a witness in any subsequent investigation or court proceeding as to what went on in that polling place.

This was a primary election: the ballot was a long one, providing for votes for Democratic and Republican candidates for president, senator, governor and member of congress, as well as a long list of those running for county offices and for judges of the municipal courts.

In our various political science classes, we had learned all about the "floating ballot," and how it worked. A blank ballot is marked by a precinct worker outside the polling place and he hands it to a voter who conceals it and goes into the polling place. He is handed a blank ballot, goes into the voting booth, puts the blank ballot in his pocket, puts the marked ballot in the ballot box on his way out and hands the blank ballot to the precinct worker to be marked again the same way. This was a game that had been going on for years in many large voting constituencies, as well as in many Chicago precincts, but the floating ballot exercise did not happen on this election day in this precinct, because it was not necessary. The voter was often accompanied by a judge or a clerk into the voting booth and "assisted" in his choices. The ballot did not need to float anywhere; control of the voting was in the polling place. The package of printed affidavits to be filled out for each assisted voter remained unopened on the front window ledge.

PARTY TIME

Larry Grandahl and I never had to go out for lunch because the back room became a sort of picnic ground, with sandwiches, large dishes of spaghetti, ravioli, and linguini with plastic utensils and paper plates and cups. Various people in the neighborhood come in to vote, or to have lunch or both. One comely, slender, black-haired Italian girl, very talkative, was there to serve food and coffee. She had a little radio nearby on a shelf, tuned to big band music, which she hummed and occasionally sang softly to herself.

By three o'clock in the afternoon, the remaining food was taken away and a half-barrel of beer was brought into the back room and set up on the table with boxes of paper cups and trays of pretzels. Voters were invited back there; most stayed only briefly, as there were few chairs and they were not encouraged to stay more than a few minutes. Individual judges and clerks would get up from their seats in the polling place and wander into the back room for some brief refreshment and conversation with each other or with friends who had come in to vote.

By about four o'clock, things began to move more quickly. Voters began to come in after the working day and the Democratic precinct workers were busy rounding up anyone in the neighborhood who could be brought in to vote. One voter came in wearing a navy topcoat; he came back about ten minutes later wearing a gray raincoat much too big for him, to vote again. I was surprised to see this attempt at changed identity because several voters during the day voted more than once without bothering to change clothes. In my report, I noted that "Corso, the judge, voted at 2:10 P.M., 2:40 P.M. and at 3:55 P.M. Saviano voted in the late afternoon and at 4:40 P.M. . . . At 5:00, the doors were closed and watcher's credentials collected . . . the judges and clerks went out to eat."

"BIG JIM" DELIVERS THE PRECINCT

Larry Grandahl and I did not go out to eat when the polling place closed, mostly because we thought we should stay with the ballots and partly because we had plenty to eat in the afternoon in the back room before it was turned into a bar. When the judges and clerks came back from their supper, James Prignano was with them. As Democratic precinct captain, he had been in and out of the polling place all day long. When he returned after supper, he was genial, as usual, and it being a chilly evening, he came in wearing a large double-breasted camel hair coat and his usual Borsalino fedora, somewhat resembling a jovial Wallace Beery in a gangland movie. He was clearly in charge of the proceedings involving the vote count and went at it with methodical efficiency, removing his coat but not his hat. It was clear that the Democratic ballots belonged to "Big Jim," the precinct captain, and to his partner and assistant captain, William Cavico.

The group in the back room was nothing if not bipartisan, for it included Anthony Mordente, the Republican precinct captain and two other Republican workers. The Democratic and Republican ballots were separated and Big Jim and Cavico sat down with the Democratic ballots in front of them on the table. Prignano had offered me money earlier in the day, taking me aside and shaking my hand. The handshake contained a roll of bills, and I had to quickly give it back to him as he started to walk away. During the evening in the back room, Mordente pressed me to accept money and wanted to know if he could help me with my college expenses. I said, "Thanks, but no, you don't need to."

What went on in that room that night has stayed with me all my life because I couldn't believe it was happening. Excerpt from my report:

> *Mr. Prignano sat down with the Democratic ballots and went through them with a pencil and eraser marking them as he saw fit. During the count, at least fifteen people handled the ballots. Cavico helped Prignano in marking the ballots. This took a couple of hours or more. Meanwhile, Corso and Morelli were tallying the Republican ballots, but they were not involved in any systematic ballot changes. The procedure followed by Prignano was to figure what the various candidates should get, mark the ballots accordingly, and inform the clerks how many marks to put after name on the tally sheets. When Mr. Prignano got through marking the Democratic ballots, it did not, therefore, take long to count them. The rest of the time until midnight was spent in tying up the ballots*

preparatory to taking them to City Hall. . . . Total votes recorded in poll book: 444. Total number of ballots: Democratic 246; Republican 198. Total number of instructed voters: between 175 and 200. Affidavits made out for instructed voters; none Number of challenged voters; 2. Number allowed to vote: 2.

The polling place was closed and the ballots sent to the City Hall. Big Jim had delivered the precinct to the Democratic organization as always. The next day I wrote my report and delivered it to Mr. McQueeny at the Association of Commerce.

TIME FOR TESTIMONY

There followed a period of several of several months when I didn't think about my work on election day. The general election in November was not monitored by any group of watchers hired by the Association of Commerce. We learned in December that State's Attorney Courtney had filed a case in county court charging the polling officials of the 31st precinct of the 20th ward with irregularities in the primary election of April 14th. I received a summons to appear as a prosecuting witness in this case before County Judge Edmund K. Jarecki.

A few days prior to my court appearance, I spent an hour with John Boyle, a Courtney assistant, who was on the case with Special Prosecutor John F. Cashen. Boyle coached me thoroughly on possible defense strategy, and how I should stay with the facts in my written report, not deviating in any detail, and that I would face tough cross-examination by Defense Attorney Charles F. Rathbun.

"Don't let him scare you," Boyle said, "just stick with the facts."

The *Chicago Daily News* on December 8, 1936, had a front page story about my testimony:

WATCHER TELLS OF ORGY OF VOTE FRAUDS IN 20TH

A description of a veritable Roman holiday at the 31st precinct of the 20th ward during the primary last April 14, with the judges and clerks and a goodly number of their friends participating in violation of practically all known election laws, was given in county court today by Samuel Hair, 5748 Kimbark Avenue, a poll watcher.

Five officials of this precinct are on trial before Judge Edmund K Jarecki. . . . Hair was a graduate student of political science at the University of Chicago . . . he said a total of 150 voters were given assistance without affidavits . . . election officials handed ballots to voters, then took the ballots back and marked them and placed them in the boxes.

TELLS OF DRINKING ORGY

"Hair testified that at 3 P.M., copious quantities of beer and whiskey arrived and a bar of sorts was established in a back room. Shortly thereafter, a number of workers emerged from the back room well drunk.

During the last forty minutes before the polls closed, Hair said, twenty-nine names were written into the poll books, although only fifteen persons voted legally . . . the extra names were furnished by one William Cavico, a Democratic worker.

> *As a climax to the festivities, Hair said, James Prignano, identified as the Democratic precinct captain, took over the Democratic ballots while the officials were counting those cast by Republicans and changed markings to suit himself."*

∼

At the trial, I had been questioned by Boyle, which brought out all of the lurid details in the *Daily News'* story. Unexpectedly, I was only briefly cross-examined by the defense attorney, Mr. Rathbun. The trial continued for a few days after my testimony. A handwriting expert was brought in, who confirmed that many erasures and marks were made by different hands on many ballots.

Because the judges and clerks were technically officers of the court, they could only be charged with contempt. Defense Attorney Rathbun's final remarks to the jury were to make several points: his clients were pure in heart and had no previous convictions; they would not knowingly break any law and if they did, it was because they were ignorant of some of the complicated rules for conducting primary elections; they deny all the charges made by Mr. Hair.

After a short deliberation, the five of Mr. Rathbun's clients were found guilty. They received one year sentences, suspended on the condition that they not serve as judges or clerks in any election for the next five years, and pay fines of $500.00 each.

THE GRAND JURY

In early January 1937, I was named in an editorial in the *Chicago Daily News*, recommending that I be summoned by the grand jury to describe what happened on election day the previous April where I was a poll watcher. (I haven't been able to retrieve a copy of the paper sixty-five years later, but I do recall its editorial message.)

Later that month, I was in a political science class at the university on the second floor of Cobb Hall. The class ended at about eleven o'clock, and as I walked out, I was approached by Bill Mather, the university registrar and a family friend, accompanied by another man.

"Sam," he said, "This is a deputy sheriff and he has a grand jury subpoena for you. You will need to talk to him."

I was not totally surprised. The deputy explained that the subpoena was dated for me to appear tomorrow, but if I wanted to appear today at two P.M., he would give me a ride out to the County Court Building on the west side and a ride home at the end of the day. If I appeared tomorrow, he said, I would have to have my own transportation. This was enough to persuade me to go with him. He went to a phone in Mather's office and called the courthouse to say that I would be there to testify at two o'clock.

It appeared to me that when the grand jury wanted a witness, they wanted the sheriff to find that witness right now. I thought I would be home by the end of the day, so I didn't call anybody. The deputy and I had a pleasant ride out to the courthouse on 26th Street at 2800 west on California Avenue, an industrial district. I was shown into a waiting area near the grand jury room, and was told also that I could go to the snack bar in the basement where I could get some quick lunch before two o'clock. I did that, and returned to the waiting room where I was called into the jury room a few minutes after two.

The grand jury room had seats for about fifty people in several rows, but the twenty-four jurors were there sitting in the two front rows, facing a lectern for me where I stood in front of them the whole time. I had no notes. I had to answer everything from memory. There was no one else in the room. The foreman in the front row had a small table in front of him with a bundle of papers on it. He was the one who swore me in and asked the first questions as to my name, occupation, and whereabouts on April 14, 1936.

Throughout my hour of testimony, the questions asked by various jury members almost always began with, "Is it true that . . . ?" and my questioner would quote directly from my written report referring to a specific incident or series of events. More than once, a jury member would say, "Did you in fact see (Mr. Prignano or Mr. Cavico) changing the marks on ballots during the vote count?"

It was almost as if they were confirming certain parts of my report, sentence by sentence, especially the creative way Prignano and Cavico marked the ballots. I was dismissed at about three thirty and driven home by the deputy sheriff. I found my grand jury experience to be much more impressive because they were not encumbered by the procedures of a courtroom with a judge and with lawyers for both sides making contending arguments. In the grand jury room, they only wanted to find out what happened that election day in that precinct. They focused on that to see if it was sufficient to justify an indictment.

The 1930s were a time when gangland corruption of Chicago's police and judges was diminishing. In the 1920s, it had been more than organized–it was institutionalized. Still, I wondered if there was any possible gangland retribution because of my courtroom testimony. Two years previously, Big Jim's brother, State Representative Al Prignano, had been gunned down by shotgun blasts as he walked from his car to the front door of his home. This was yet another of the many unsolved Chicago murders by "persons unknown."

I ventured to ask John Boyle, "Is anybody going to come after me or my family because of my testimony?"

He quickly replied, "No. They only kill each other. If they ever come after somebody like you, there's hell to pay, and they know it. Don't worry about it." He was right. We never had any even remote indication that there would be any reprisal.

THE FULL CIRCLE

My part in the final act of the vote fraud drama came in December 1937, and my appearance as the main witness for State's Attorney Courtney in the criminal court of Judge Rudolph Desort. This was not only a trial of Prignano, but also Mordente and Cavico. The three were charged with "conspiring to alter ballots." My testimony was pretty much a repeat of much that I had said in previous testimony in the county court of Judge Jarecki. The trial went on for several days and my recollection of its conclusion is that the three were convicted, sentenced to one-year prison terms and fined $1000.00 each. Big Jim could no longer be a precinct captain, but he remained an important figure in the Democratic organization and in the Italian community.

Professor Charles E. Merriam, the political science department head at the university, had been following the court cases in which I was involved. He told me in one of our conversations that I had probably given the final push to a tottering edifice–the use of the paper ballot in Chicago and Cook County. There was some resistance to its replacement with voting machines, which were said to be too expensive. The resistance came mainly from precinct workers, accomplished in the use of the floating ballot, and who would now have to deliver the vote by delivering the voters. The voting machines came anyway, and all these years after that election day in 1936, the Democratic organization in Chicago is still alive and well.

V. THE ROCK

The Galapagos Archipelago is one of the most desolate and barren places in the world. For the most part, the islands are unhabitable due to the lack of fresh water and rough terrain. There are ten principal islands and many smaller ones. The formation of the whole group is volcanic. Craters with geologically recent lava flows cover most of the islands, giving them a remarkable similarity in appearance. Each island has one or more central craters rising as high as 4,500 feet with rocky ridges and glacier-like lava formations sloping to the shore. The Galapagos iguana and giant land tortoise are the best known of the local species of wildlife and are found only on these islands. The Ecuadorian government has prohibited hunting or acquisition of these animals. The Naval Auxiliary Air Facility is located on Seymore (Baltra) Island adjoining Santa Cruz on the north.

—History of Patrol Squadron One
Samuel C. Hair, Lt. (jg) USNR
Historical Officer
28 December 1944

HOW I GOT THERE

My draft card was dated November 12, 1941. It was from Selective Service, and said, "The person named herein whose order number is 2557 has been classified by Local Board in Class 1-A until further notice." It was a postcard, and "the person named herein" was my name on the address side of the card.

I knew I could wait until they sent me orders to report somewhere, or I could try to get into some kind of officer training. My instincts were to try the Navy first. This was partly because one of my close friends in high school, Russell Dell, had gone on to the Naval Academy. He never failed to call me on his visits to Chicago when he came home to visit his parents. A few weeks previously, we had spent an evening together, and in one of our more serious conversations, he had said, "Stay out of the Army if you can, Sam. The Navy is different, and probably better."

He went on to remind me that President Roosevelt had been Assistant Secretary of the Navy, that the Army and Navy Departments were supposed to be equal, but the Navy Department was "more equal," and was more influential in the Congress. So, the next week I went downtown to the Board of Trade Building on Jackson Boulevard, where Navy and Marine recruiting offices were, and signed up for V-5, aviation training in the Navy. I was twenty-six, the upper age limit for acceptance into that program.

That was only the preliminary step to my reporting the next day to the Navy Pier, a large assemblage of offices and medical facilities, jutting out in to Lake Michigan near the foot of the Chicago River. My physical exam included an eye test, which I failed, as 20-20 vision was required and I didn't quite have it. I thought that failing the test had ended my Navy career before it began, but the examining doctor said, "If you want to, you can come back and take the eye exam again five days from now, and I won't put you down for failing it today. Sometimes the results are better if you don't go to any movies, don't do a lot of reading, and get a lot of rest."

I said, "Thanks, I'll be back." I left there in early afternoon, and managed to see Dr. McBean, whose office was downtown not far away. He was a family friend, and the ophthalmologist we all went to. When I got to his office, his receptionist said he was too busy to see me, but I convinced her it was a matter of my naval career and national security, and I was able to get in to see him after waiting about an hour. He listened carefully to my story, and then gave me much the same advice I had received from the Navy eye doctor: "Don't read much, no movies, go to bed early, and here are some eye drops to take every night before your Navy exam."

The second time I took the eye test, I passed with 20-20 vision, thanks to Dr. McBean. I was given a mimeographed form saying that I was now in the Navy, that I would receive orders at an unspecified future date, and that I shouldn't leave town. December 7, 1941, was only a couple of weeks away. After that memorable day, I knew I'd hear from the Navy and where they wanted me to go. I did indeed hear from them in late December, but only to tell me that I would receive orders to report to Glenview Naval Air Station, north of Chicago, but that I was not to report until April 15 next, my 27th birthday. It seems that Glenview NAS was still being built, and so were the N3N training planes ("Yellow Peril") built on a Stearman pattern, and coming from the Naval Aircraft Factory. By April, the Glenview NAS would be ready with enough airplanes to be in business. In V-5 we would be enlisted as Seamen 2nd Class, be paid $30.00 per month, and begin primary training of eleven hours of instruction leading to solo flying, and a few maneuvers such as small-field lands and recovery from spins. Those completing the program would go to Pensacola, Corpus Christie, or Jacksonville for advanced training, where we would become Aviation Cadets.

In November 1941, my friend Russell Dell, soon to become a lieutenant (jg), was ordered to the USS *Edsall*, a destroyer stationed in the Philippines. After Pearl Harbor, he saw action in the Asiatic-Pacific area, and in mid-March his parents were notified that he was "Officially determined to be MISSING IN ACTION as of 1 March 1942, having been serving aboard the USS *Edsall* when that ship was lost due to enemy action in the vicinity of Java . . ."

In the interval between December 7 and March 1, he had already been awarded the Philippine Defense Ribbon with one bronze star, the Asiatic-Pacific Area Campaign Medal with two bonze stars, and the Purple Heart. He was one of many in the Navy who were involved in continuing enemy action in that area immediately after Pearl harbor. The USS *Edsall* went down with all hands. The Secretary of the Navy and the President of the United States sent their condolences to his parents. When I heard about it, I visited his mother at their apartment on 72nd Street near the lake. She knew me as a close friend of the family, and impressed me with her brave demeanor, and acceptance of the loss of her oldest boy. She said, "Well, Sam, we had him for twenty-seven years and we're so very proud of him . . ."

A recapitulation of the time at the Glenview Naval Air Station was best described in later years by Boyce McCoy, who reported there with me in April of 1942. We kept up a correspondence, and in 1996, fifty-four years later, in one of his letters he brought back some of the Glenview experiences:

Dear Sambo,

Your letter brings to mind our time, yours and mine, in *our war*. Memories of December 7th, even at this late date, remain crystal clear. In the middle of that Sunday afternoon, I was suffering from the rigors of a lively Saturday night, when the sportscast of the Bears' football game was interrupted by the news announcement of the attack on Pearl Harbor. Obviously, the jig was up—I was destined to be in uniform, probably sooner than somewhat. An old friend of the family convinced me that the war was going to be a long one, and that I should try to enlist in an activity that might teach me something, and where I would be in the company of some good guys for the next several years.

So, in company with thirty-odd other fledglings, possessed of the necessary college credits, physically qualified, and formally sworn in, you and I reported for duty as Seamen 2/c, V5, at the Naval Reserve Aviation base in nearby Glenview on April 15, 1942. For the first six weeks, we had nothing but close-order marching drill, calisthenics, and all-day sessions of ground school included minutely-detailed lectures on the mysteries and joys of addition, subtraction, long division, decimals and fractions.

In early June, we began flying in N3Ns, similar to Stearmans, but produced at the Naval Aircraft Factory and a little slower (65 knots). First, Stage "A," learning the rudimentary skills necessary for soloing—takeoffs, climbs, glides, turns and landings—45 minutes daily or until the Navy decided to gamble on letting us solo. Finally, they declared me safe, to my surprise, and I was allowed several solo flights.

Then came Stage "B" at a grass auxiliary field—"S" turns to full-stall precision landings in the landing circle, and slipping the airplane into the circle. In this latter maneuver, I slipped the airplane's left wingtip into the ground, the plane flipping over and coming to a quick halt. We were upside down hanging on our seatbelts. My 21-year-old instructor, Ensign Guy, displayed his distress, muttering, "You can do better than this, McCoy."

Flight checks for each stage were entrusted solely to senior instructors—one was Captain Prall, a Marine of particularly stern demeanor. On a memorable occasion, Prall flew a student to Site Nine, a practice field near Arlington Heights, got out of the plane and took a position just outside the landing circle. Sitting on his parachute, he was now ready to critique the student's attempts at making "S" turns and sideslips into the circle.

The student then took off. On the first try, he made the "S" turns adroitly, but on attempting to slip into the circle, an element of smallfield landing practice, he missed the circle and headed directly for Captain Prall who scrambled to his feet and ran for his life.

The cadet landed outside the circle then took off again to make another attempt. He climbed to the stipulated 600 feet, but before he could make another pass at the circle, a black thunderstorm burst forth. Complying with long-standing firm orders for solo students, he headed immediately back to the main station, abandoning the unhappy and damp Marine captain to the elements. It was said that Captain Prall's relationship to that student became intractable; the student, however, claimed he was following orders, so they gave him another instructor. The Navy needed pilots.

Concrete runways had not yet been built at Glenview, which was only a large grass field with a windsock to indicate the landing direction. At the close of one flight period, there was a sudden 180 degree change in the wind direction. As the last of ten N3Ns came in landing north, another ten came in landing south. Ensign Bell, the duty officer, ran about wildly shouting and firing a Very Pistol as fast as he could reload it to warn the planes in the air to go around again. The warning was too late, but the astonishment of everyone, they all landed without a collision or even a brushed wingtip–a remarkable achievement in aviation training history.

There was one of the cadets who was especially singled out for his fanatical infatuation with his aviation career, to the exclusion of everything else in his life. Most of us believed this early part of aviation training to be something we had to go through to become commissioned officers, so we put up with it and did just enough to pass the ground school courses; we did give serious efforts to learn the mysteries of airplanes and how to fly them. Ron Gilgenbach, however, could only think and talk about whatever phase of the program he was involved in at the moment, and tell us all how exciting and wonderful it was. "God, this is so great!" he would say to any of us who would listen. He frequently accompanied such remarks with a big smile and a high-pitched whinnying laugh, which led us to begin to call him "Giggle-ass."

Our dormitory was connected to a recreation room, containing a couple of sofas, some straight chairs and card tables, and a shelf on one wall where there was a radio and a wind-up phonograph, which would play 78 rpm records. Gilgenbach had a recording of a song celebrating naval aviation, and entitled "Sky Anchors Aweigh." After Glenview, I never heard that song again anywhere in the Navy because no one liked it, and the Navy never adopted it as its aviation "fight song." The recording was brassy and contained many verses sung by a large male chorus. Most of us hated it. But Gilgenbach would wind up the phonograph, stand close to it, and play "Sky Anchors Aweigh" not once but several times, totally attentive, and wearing a dreamy smile. The only way to get him out of this trance was to shout, "Hey. Giggle-ass, turn that damn thing off!"

He would reluctantly do so, not understanding why we all didn't share his reverence for this musical tribute to our careers.

McCoy's letter goes on to describe the dormitory where we cadets slept in rows of double-deck bunks, and where we each had a nearby locker containing all our worldly goods. Lights went out at ten o'clock, and an officer with a flashlight passed down the rows to see if we were all indeed tucked in. When he had confirmed this, he was gone until six in the morning, when the lights went on and reveille was sounded over the speaker system.

Lights out in the dormitory meant that McCoy's basso profundo voice would begin to lead us in a chorus of songs derived from traditional melodies but with original words. Fred Waring, plus the Mormon Tabernacle, might have been envious:

> Oh, it's moonlight every night at Glenview,
> And every night is summertime.
> For there's more food fellows out at Glenview
> Than any base the wide world o'er.
> You won't hear Caruso out at Glenview,
> But all the boys sing fine.
> And it's moonlight every night at Glenview,
> And every night is summertime.

Gilgenbach never took offense at his new nickname; he remained good-natured and may even have enjoyed being so singled out. He went on to continue training at Corpus Christie, and become a scout-bomber pilot with a squadron that saw action in the Pacific. Others in our group at Glenview were not so fortunate. Two were "washed out" because they got sick in any kind of plane maneuver such as steep descents or sharp turns. This made it impossible for them to go forward into aerobatics, so they were given medical discharges, and options to apply for other officer-candidate programs, or to stay in as Seamen 2c and train to be aviation machinist mates. They both opted for another OCS program.

The conclusion of McCoy's letter goes on:

After three-and-a-half months we were promoted to advanced training at Jacksonville, Florida, leaving the Seaman 2c rating and the $30.00 per month pay scale behind us. We could now wear "blues," the Navy dress uniform, but without any stripes. We mostly wore the Navy khakis with brown shoes, to distinguish us from line officers who wore black shoes.

At JAX NAS they put us through much of the same ground school all over again. Then we got into celestial navigation, but not the theory, only the solutions to problems involving spherical trigonometry, and how to take sights with an octant of the stars, moon, and sun, and put these measurements into a book of tables called H.O.214. This was to give us the plane's position, but we were told also to keep careful dead-reckoning record by keeping track of time, true heading, and ground speed.

We began at JAX flying Stearmans in Stage C–aerobatics. These were wingovers, slow rolls, snap rolls, Immelman turns, loops, and the "split S." We enjoyed snap rolls because they were over in a hurry. One maneuver we didn't enjoy was the inverted spin and how to recover from it. The instructors didn't enjoy this either, but were required to show us, one time and one time only, after climbing to 8,000 feet and making sure our seat belts were securely fastened. This is a maneuver in which, if you ever stall into one, you can lose a lot of altitude in a hurry. Prompt recovery is required to survive it.

After "C" Stage, we went on the little Ryan NR-1 monoplanes, North American SNJ's for instrument training, Vought OS2U's for formation flying, before going into the final squadron, Consolidated PY's—in total, the nearly nine months comprised 230 hours. The advice from my family friend to get into Naval Aviation was right on target.

We formed solid friendships with many wonderful guys that have endured over fifty years. A gratifying experience in every sense of the word.

All good wishes,
Boyce

There came a time in aviation training, after being checked out in the SNJ for instrument instruction, when we were given a choice: to continue training in scout bombers and fighters, or to go into multi-engine patrol planes. The latter were the four-engine PB4Y (known in the Army as the B-24), and two different seaplanes—the four-engine PB2Y, and the twin engine PBY. The PBY turned out to be ubiquitous in World War II combat areas, performing successfully some desperate missions for which it had never been designed. The PBY2Y was not produced in large numbers by Consolidated Aircraft, and was frequently used as a utility plane for cargo and transport, and for antisubmarine patrol in the South Atlantic. Two squadrons of PB2Ys were stationed and saw enemy action in the Pacific.

I was given my commission as an ensign, and my wings as a Naval Aviator, January 12, 1943, along with twenty others in my group. we were given leave, and ordered to report back ten days later. I went to Waterville, Maine, to visit my sister and her husband. He was an executive of the Hathaway Shirt Company, in charge of manufacturing. Since the military was taking their entire production, Van, my brother-in-law, was deferred from military service. He didn't really like that, but did his best to keep the factory running two shifts making shirts for the Army.

When I left Waterville, I was one of many in uniform by this time, giving me priority for train travel back to Jacksonville NAS for operational training in the PBY for three months. This led to my being qualified as a multi-engine seaplane pilot, and orders to report to NAS Norfolk, Virginia, the headquarters of the Atlantic Fleet, where I would be given orders to active duty.

About a dozen of us from Jacksonville arrived one morning at the NAS Administration Building for our squadron assignments. We formed lines at 0900 in May in front of two windows in a large room, one marked "A to M," the other "N to Z," rather like bank tellers' windows, with a petty officer behind each one, seated there with a pile of orders to be handed out. When I arrived at the window and gave my name and serial number, the petty officer shuffled through a pile of papers, and handed me my orders with a "Thank you, sir." Those of us who had come in together waited until we all had received our orders, so that we could walk back in a group to the BOQ, and compare our destinies on active duty in The Fleet.

My orders were to join Patrol Squadron ONE at Coco Solo, Panama. The man ahead of me was ordered to a squadron in Perth, Australia; the man behind me was ordered to Goose Bay, Labrador. It was clear that the aviation cadet training schools at Jacksonville, Corpus Christie, and Pensacola were turning out naval aviators to serve in many places in the Free World, but we were given no choice as to where that might be. Our orders were marked "Confidential," and we had been cautioned not to tell any family members or anyone else outside the Navy where we were going. Families and others could reach us only by mail addressed to "Fleet Post Office, New York, NY."

When I got to Coco Solo, by way of NATS from Miami on May 23, and reported to the Senior Naval Aviator, Squadron VP-1, I quickly learned that this was not a PBY squadron; it was a squadron of four-engine PBY2Y's, the largest seaplane in the Navy. Of the fifty pilots assigned to it, a few had been checked out in this larger plane in San Diego, but all the others reporting in from aviation cadet training had to go through a shake-down, pre-operational training period to become first pilots in the PB2Y. It was not until October that the squadron became operational as a part of Fleet Air Wing Three, and began routine anti-submarine and convoy coverage flights in the South Atlantic, where the Germans were then very active: shipping losses were frequent and serious. In January 1944, we learned that VP-1 was to be moved within a few weeks to be based in the Galapagos, at Aeolian Bay, the protected harbor of Seymour Island.

A RARE MOMENT THAT OCCURRED DURING THE WAR . . . JANUARY, 1944

I went into the officers' club at Coco Solo one hot night to drink beer, was sitting at the bar and Ned Bartlett tapped me on the shoulder. He was a Deke from Chicago, class of 1937, a football player . . . backfield on one of the last Big Ten teams before Hutchins abolished football. I hadn't seen him since then since he lived in Glendale, CA. Next day I went to see him on his brand new DE (destroyer escort) anchored at the submarine base, and he took me all around it. He was its executive officer. He was leaving early next morning to go through the Canal to the Pacific. Next morning I took off in a PB2Y at daybreak, and just before we left the water I could see Ned's ship putting out to Manzanillo Bay from its berth at the docks, he going one way, I going out to cover a convoy. But it seemed symbolic of so many things that happened during those years—the DE pushing out into the bay at full speed with an old college friend of mine on board, and I could just see his ship for a minute or two, brave and new, while we were taking off with the outrageous noise of our four engines at full throttle. "So long, Ned," I thought, " and watch yourself." I heard from him later, about three months later—a long letter. His ship had had the full treatment at Ulithi, Okinawa, Iwo Jima. Some day I'll stop and see him again in Glendale. He'd be there. But I never have.

WHY WE WERE THERE

The Galapagos was the site of one of three NAAF (Naval Auxiliary Air Facility) stations in that area of the eastern Pacific in WWII. The other two were at Corinto, Nicaragua and Salinas, Ecuador. They were to provide facilities for seaplane patrol tracks covering the Pacific sea lanes leading to the Panama Canal to identify merchant shipping. The patrols were considered a fundamental security measure for the Panama Sea Frontier. This was a circle about 500 nautical miles out from the Canal and all shipping in that area had to be identified as to nationality, destination, owner, and cargo.

When the Navy established NAAF, it did so with thoroughness. Each of the three had facilities for 100 officers and 500 to 600 enlisted men and was departmentalized into operations, communications, ordnance, engine overhaul and commissary and was, in effect, a small Naval Air Station. Our squadron at the Galapagos was there to fly the tracks to and from Corinto, a round trip requiring two days with a nine-hour flight each day and an overnight stop at Corinto.

SEYMOUR ISLAND

There are several islands in the world called "The Rock." Two that come to mind are Ascension and Alcatraz. Ascension is a British possession in the middle of the Atlantic Ocean, about eight degrees south of the equator and about halfway between Brazil and the west African coast. Alcatraz was a federal prison in San Francisco Bay.

Seymour Island in the Galapagos is one of the smallest islands in that archipelago, but has a natural protected harbor, Aeolian Bay, suitable for a seaplane landing area. Those of us in VP-1 (Patrol Squadron One) flying PBY and PB2Y Navy flying boats called Seymour Island "The Rock."

Each of the Islands of the Galapagos has two names, British and Spanish, the first given by a British nautical survey in 1836, the second by the Ecuadorian government in later years. "Seymour" is the British name for The Rock, "Baltra," the Spanish. It is a small island separated from the north side of a large island, Indefatigable, of Santa Cruz, by the narrow Itabacca Channel.

The Galapagos in the WWII years had no tourists. They hadn't discovered it yet in large numbers, and wartime restrictions were in effect anyway.

Seymour Island is about ten miles long from north to south and less than half that from east to west. The harbor of protected water, Aeolian Bay, is on the northwest end and the Navy buildings were on gently rising ground above the harbor and the seaplane ramp and hanger. The southeast, or windward side, is a steep cliff, battered by waves coming in from miles out and crashing against it. The opposite, or leeward side, is partly a beautiful, wide white sand beach about a mile long, fronting on the calm ocean with gentle swells and small waves and easily accessible from the Navy installation by Jeep or a twenty minute walk.

Soon after Pearl Harbor, Army engineers built a 5,000 foot runway for Air Force planes, but the Navy installation was by far larger. It was put there by the CB's (Construction Battalions) with several Quonset huts, a large frame open hangar where one plane could be beached and serviced. On a hill overlooking Aeolian Bay was the dispensary and the "wine mess" (navy for Officer's Club). At a lower level were barracks and a mess hall for our fifty pilots and forty other officers, barracks and mess hall for 500 enlisted men, and a club building for them. There was a building accommodating the other parts of a Navy squadron organization, including communications, training, gunnery, engineering and commissary. There was also an open air movie theater with a shelter at the rear for the projectionist and a stage up front for the screen and the sound equipment. Many rows of wooden benches were arranged in a semi-circle in front of the screen to accommodate about 500 men. Seating was not comfortable, but the movies were well attended. Somehow we saw recent Hollywood productions often featuring Betty Grable or Rita Hayworth brought in by plane, Army or Navy, from Panama.

The officers' wine mess building had a bar where drinks were thirty-five cents, including several favorite brands of Scotch, which most of us drank. There were several card tables and a full-size pool table used for pool during the day and for and ongoing crap game beginning about nine o'clock every night. Our skipper, a regular navy man of deep wisdom and experience, ordered the bar

1944–Sam at the Rock

closed and the dice game to end at eleven o'clock. He knew that if he didn't, even though we were "officers and gentlemen," it was sound judgment to limit these temptations on a lonely place like The Rock. He did not put an end to the serious poker games that went on in the barracks when the wine mess was closed. He knew it would be difficult so he didn't try.

When the CBs were building the NAAF Galapagos, they knew the island had few recreational facilities so a tennis court was included in their plans. They built an asphalt pad after bulldozing enough space for it on a rocky hillside with a wire fence at either end for backstops. The net was a chain-link fence about three feet high with no sag in the middle and hung on iron posts on each side. The court lines were painted white with a thick brush on each side of the net but with some imagination as to the exact measurements on the plans. However, their measurements were close and it was possible to play tennis on The Rock. One problem was racquets and balls, but slowly, we accumulated a few racquets and balls brought in from officers' clubs in Panama. Tennis balls were used until they were smooth and almost black from the asphalt and bounced only reluctantly, but then tennis at The Rock was accepted as being "different."

I managed to carry my tennis racquet to some of the places to which I was assigned. When I got orders to go to the Canal Zone, I knew they had everything so I took my racquet there but left it when we were sent to advanced bases such as The Rock. When I found, on my first visit, that in the NAAF Galapagos there was a tennis court, I had the next plane from Coco Solo bring my racquet from my quarters at the BOQ there.

I played often with Doctor Ed Goodman, our flight surgeon. We had many spirited games of singles on this hot asphalt tennis court with the wire net. He was from New York City, a highly trained surgeon in his mid-thirties and occasionally monumentally bored because he had nothing to do. He took up watercolor painting and would spend hours with a sketch pad at various parts of the island doing coastal scenes and seascapes. He was sometimes busy treating enlisted men returning from a liberty party in Managua. Usually, about half a group of thirty returning from a two-day visit to Nicaragua's capital city would return with gonorrhea, which would show up about a week later and require a visit to Dr. Goodman's dispensary. He realized that treating these cases was a job that "somebody has to do." His surgical skill was not unknown elsewhere. On one occasion a destroyer enroute to New Guinea anchored in the harbor with a man on board suffering from the late stages of peritonitis. Dr. Goodman came out in the crash boat, took the young man ashore and operated on him in the dispensary up on the hill. The ship went on without him and the man was flown back to Panama to a hospital. He later joined the crew of another destroyer.

THE OTHER END OF THE TRACK

The town of Corinto didn't offer much then and probably doesn't now. It was typical of many Nicaraguan villages in that it had unpaved streets, a large Catholic church, a few bars frequented by Navy personnel, and a couple of restaurants with very limited native menus and equally limited sanitation. No one in Corinto owned a car. The only motor vehicles were small trucks going to and from the harbor and the ubiquitous Navy Jeeps. There is a large railroad station with ancient steam trains carrying both passengers and freight between Managua on the east and Chinandega on the west. The harbor was the busiest place and the harbor master the most important man in the town. He was also related to the Somoza family. Corinto was not a deep water seaport so the vessels coming in to the docks were small freighters at high tide. The next most important man in the town and probably the wealthiest, was the British agent. He had charge of the warehouses and shelters near the harbor, the docks filled with imported goods to go to Managua, and any exported native products ready to be loaded and shipped out. He lived in a two-acre compound facing the ocean outside the town, protected by a high chain link fence. In the compound was a commodious frame house with a wide front porch, a few utility sheds, a generator for electricity, and a stable with two saddle horses, all surrounded by carefully tended tropical gardens. The Somozas were his friends.

The British agent had a daughter whom we knew only by sight. We think she lived in London and came home to Corinto at Christmas and Easter. I saw her briefly once when I was walking on the dirt road from our base to the town. She came riding along at a brisk trot on a handsome bay horse. She looked to be about twenty or younger, and was wearing the female equestrian garb one might see on a fox hunt, including boots and jodhpurs, hard visored hat, and riding crop. She came trotting toward me and we passed without saying a word. I never saw her again. It was plain that she had no interest in hanging out with Navy people. I think the chances are she spent more time in London with her mother and was in school there.

TEMPORARY DUTY IN THE PBY

I learned in January 1944 that I was to be assigned as a pilot to the crew of a PBY flying the north-south tracks between The Rock and Corinto. I was one of three pilots, the other two being Lt. (jg) Welby ("Whip") Williams and ENS W. S. ("Bill") Young. Whip was senior to us and the PPC (Patrol Plane Commander). He was an engaging, talkative Texan and a veteran of combat in the western Pacific with VP-33. He had a natural aptitude for flying, was careful and thorough as was I, and he wanted to know all about the airplane he was flying: the engine hours, last overhaul, and other details mostly taken for granted by the other pilots in our squadron. Most of all, he was cheerful with a reasonable cynicism about the Navy and its chauvinistic ways and traditions. The three of us were together from January 20 to February 17.

I look back on this as the most enjoyable and unstructured, stress-free period in my time on active duty in the Navy. It was not quite like a holiday or a vacation because we had to make several nine-hour flights on the zig-zag tracks between The Rock and Corinto. At the end of every flight we reported in at the communications desk as to all the shipping observed and that was all. During that month we were together, the weather was clear, the sea calm and we saw many whales; occasionally we circled around at 150 feet to see them better. When we were ashore, there was no eight o'clock morning muster. We had to fly from The Rock to Corinto, stay overnight, fly back to The Rock the next day, and do it again two or three days later.

One squadron was to be entirely composed of the larger four engine PB2Y-3, so our use of the twin engine PBY was temporary and came to an end when the three of us were ordered back to the main base at Coco Solo in February. The PBY was no longer used on a regular basis for The Rock–Corinto tracks, and our temporary duty was over. We accepted this as a matter of inevitability, but we also knew it meant returning to a pool of fifty pilots assigned to different crews on each flight, a prospect not as alluring as our time away by ourselves the previous month.

THE GOOD LIFE ON THE ROCK

I have always been fascinated by The Rock and the Galapagos in general. It never rained, the air was so clear and dry that I could wash my shirts, underwear, and socks in the morning, hang them up in the sun and they would be dry by mid-afternoon. Navy pilots, like most military men, are not easily impressed by anything, or if they are, they conceal it with the usual macho cynicism. I could tell that my fifty pilot companions here were curious and sometimes even amazed at what they could see in this obscure, primitive place. We found ourselves to be together in one of the world's unique spots. As pilots, we were all put together in our own barracks, several frame buildings each with four small bedrooms and one bath; each bedroom had a double-deck bunk, a table and two chairs. There was no town to go to and the only night life was the movie or the officer's club for cards, dice, or drinking. The usual flying schedule for us was two days of flying the Corinto tracks and then two or three days off. We had to make an eight o'clock muster at the hangar with all hands when the flight crews would be assigned for the next day. After that, we found life on The Rock to be as busy or as lazy as we could ever prefer.

We could go to the ordnance shack and check out Springfield bolt action .303 rifles with a box of cartridges for each and go to the windward side of the island where the commissary had fashioned a wooden chute slanting off the cliff for all the garbage and trash to be dumped into the ocean. The local shark population knew about this. There were dozens of them that quickly appeared whenever anything was coming down out of the chute and we would fire away at them with our Springfields for target practice and for our own amusement.

Another pastime was to form an expedition of pilots and enlisted men to go over to Big Daphne Island, about half an hour away by Navy whaleboat. Big Daphne is a crater about three miles in diameter jutting up about five hundred feet out of the water with steep slanting rocky sides. Our whaleboat could not tie up anywhere so the boat's helmsman would maneuver it next to an area where we could scramble out, one by one, on the rocks and climb up the rugged slope, covered with bushes and cactus, to the top of the crater. The helmsman told us that he would come back in an hour to pick us up at the same place. Big Daphne is nothing but a gigantic nest for a variety of the blue-footed booby, found only on that island, in that crater. My visit there was at the time of year when there were hundreds of these large white gulls nesting all over the island on the upper edge of the crater. The interior of the crater is about a mile across, a couple of hundred feet deep, dry and hellishly hot. The birds nesting on its edge were in their own natural incubator. They had no fear of us and wouldn't move even if we gently prodded them with our feet. The only living creatures on Big Daphne were many different kinds of birds–the gulls we saw nesting there; finches of a particular variety described by Darwin, and probably found only on that island; and others that looked to be different kinds of hawks, doves, and cormorants. The island is typical of many others in this remote archipelago, most with individual varieties of wildlife, each species differing from one island to the next. Darwin was there for thirty-four days (September 16 to October 20, 1835) on the famous five year voyage of *The Beagle*. His voluminous notes on what he saw in the Galapagos led him to his heretical conclusion in *The Origin Of Species*, which changed the whole structure of modern biology.

Trip to "Big Daphne"

We did not visit any of the larger islands and consequently did not see any of the turtles for which the islands are named. They are still there in large numbers, protected by the government, and no longer a source of food for the crews of whaling ships, who, for over a hundred years, came ashore and killed them by the thousands. We did see some other forms of native wildlife, the sea iguana and his smaller relative, the land iguana. The latter we found all over our island where civilization had not encroached on their lairs. They lived in holes in rocky areas and mostly enjoyed sunning themselves for a large part of the day. They were totally unafraid of us. If one or us grabbed an iguana by the tail and pulled it off the ground, it would hang there, wriggling and looking reproachfully at its captor.

The Galapagos longusta is a large, edible marine crustacean living among the rocks in the tide pools near the shore. They could be easily retrieved at low tide and were there in such large numbers that we could wade out a few feet and spear them in the shallows or even reach down and pick up the smaller ones. The flesh of the longusta is in its body, not the claws, and tastes much like lobster. We would retrieve a dozen or so and carry them in buckets of sea water to the galley where our cooks prepared them for dinner for those who caught them. One of our group, Bob Alford, was from Ogunquit, Maine and knew about lobsters. He was able to assist our cooks in the officers' mess in the preparation of this delicacy which we could have as often as we wanted to go out and bring longustas in.

Another favorite pastime of off-duty pilots was to visit the beautiful wide white sand beach near the northeast end of the bay on the leeward side of The Rock. Sometimes as many as eight of us would crowd on to our one and only Jeep and drive the two miles to this mile-long expanse of pristine sand gently sloping away from the higher rocks down to the gentle Pacific waters on that side of the island. It was hot there, but the air was dry and enervating and the Humboldt Current kept the water cool. It was almost as if this was yet another attraction put there for us on The Rock in addition to the climate, the serenity of the surroundings, and the fascinating wildlife. A resort hotel would have been successful here but would also have effectively vandalized this corner of a primeval world. We could only be temporary visitors.

The Beach

IN HACK

I was more given to exploration to the more remote areas of The Rock than were my companions. At the other end of the track, Corinto, I was also more interested than they were in exploring the town and the harbor. I also took many photos. When I finished a roll of film in my trusty folding Kodak, I would put it away in my flight bag to hold until I could get it processed the next time I was on leave in the States. I learned the hard way that taking snapshots of certain areas and subjects was forbidden and would be censored and reported to my commanding officer if processed when we were Stateside. A roll of my film processed by a photo store in Colon, our squadron base, was censored because I had taken a few photos of machine gun emplacements on The Rock. I thought nothing about this at the time I took the pictures because the prospects of Seymour Island being invaded by the Japanese seemed remote and I attached no confidentiality to that subject. I was guilty of photographing a military installation; security within the panama Sea Frontier was exceptionally thorough. Our skipper felt that he had to go by the book and punish me in some way, so he put me "in hack," Navy for "confined to quarters," for two days and asked me to be more careful about what I was doing with my camera. He even said I could go to the officers' mess at mealtime with the others. I spent my time in hack in or near the barracks, reading paperback books, writing letters, and talking to off-duty friends who came to visit or to work up a poker game.

DR. GOODMAN

Dr. Goodman's boredom with his assignment to The Rock and his complaints about how much of his job involved treating headaches, common colds, minor cuts and bruises and venereal diseases came to a sudden and stunning end July 17, 1944.

In the late afternoon to that day, one of our four engine PB2Y-3 Coronado seaplanes crashed in Aeolian Bay, killing two of the pilots and three in the crew. There were four survivors; one pilot and three crew members, thrown clear and badly injured.

Navy seaplane hulls and airframes are made of aluminum and are not designed for landing on the water with speed and power. The landing doctrine for these large multi-engine aircraft is to bring them in slowly and when almost on the water, cut the power and drop in at a full stall. The accident report, a few days later by Charley Bardwell, our flight officer, was based largely on my testimony as a pilot and as one of the few witnesses of the whole event. On that afternoon, I happened to be on a hill near our barracks retrieving some of my laundry hung out there to dry when the plane came in for landing, returning from a typical flight covering one of our tracks. Part of the report follows:

> *Plane returned to base after routine patrol of nine hours and 25 minutes. Contact was not made with the tower and instead of circling the area, the plane made a long straight approach to the landing area in the outer bay. It is believed, from the statements of competent observers, that the landing was made downwind at a fast speed in comparison to normal landings. Plane touched the water with power on; the nose dug in suddenly and the tail lifted into the air to the perpendicular then went over disappearing into the water. The nose section was sheared off, the wing remained afloat and was subsequently salvaged. All survivors were either trapped in wreckage or thrown clear and when rescued ten minutes after the crash were either on the wing or in the water nearby . . . those killed in the accident were Lieut. W. D. Cauthan; Lieut. (jg) M. D. Scott; ARM1cc H. T. Rogers; ARM3c P. J. Crimmings and AOM2c D. K. Reed. Survivors were Lieut. (JG) F. G. Coffield; AMM1c J. H. Ainscough' AMM1c A. Cucco and AMM2c V. P. Schreiner. The survivors sustained serious injuries.*

The plane now lies in forty fathoms of water about two miles off the northwest tip of Aeolian Bay. There were some attempts to locate the sunken wreckage with Navy small boats and grappling hooks, but these were unsuccessful. We had a destroyer enroute west to the Philippines stop over long enough to drop depth charges over the estimated position of the wreckage in an attempt to raise it, but that didn't work, either. A day later, the body of D. K. Reed was washed ashore, possibly as a result of depth charging. After that, the salvage effort was abandoned. Reed was buried in a grave on the hill on the east side of the harbor.

When I saw the plane come in fast, I knew it was coming in to land with power, with the pilot probably intending to take it on a fast taxi to tie up at the buoy near the shore, rather than to circle into the wind, do a slow approach to a full stall landing and taxi slowly to the buoy. The noise of the props told me that the plane hit the water with power, certainly not a full stall with power off. Two seconds later, the nose went under, the propellers and the wing were under water, the fuselage and the tail were vertically up in the air, and all was silent. Slowly everything sank except the wing without its engines, which were sheared off on impact with the water. I frantically ran down to the dock but the crash boat had already gone. I was shocked and horrified that one of our big Coronado flying boats could come to such an end.

The crash boat was at the scene in about ten minutes, the four survivors taken aboard and rushed back to the dock. Each man was put onto a canvas stretcher and carried by two men up the hill to the dispensary. Dr. Goodman was there waiting with his staff, which consisted of one corpsman and a medic trained in the fundamentals of pharmacology and first aid. So far in their Navy careers they had had no similar experience. Navy dispensaries in wartime are fully equipped for emergencies of all kinds and Dr. Goodman was grateful for this. But it was a dispensary, not a hospital, and he had only two beds and an operating table for the four critically injured men so two were laid out on blankets on the floor.

He worked quickly and carefully, just to keep their life signs going. He let me see the victims when I went up there before he had done all the multiple splints and bandages. They were all unconscious but still breathing and looked to be terribly cut up and bloody. I didn't stay long because I realized he probably wanted me out of the way. I asked him if I could do anything. He didn't answer because he was too busy, so I left. He worked all that night on the survivors and well into the next day without coming to the mess hall. When he did show up for lunch the second day, he was showing exhaustion but also exhibited a careful optimism because the four were still alive.

On that second day, I was the senior naval aviator as the pilots outranking me were out flying regular tracks and the captain and executive officer were flying to Panama to report the loss of the plane to the wing commander, who had also requested a report of the condition of the survivors. So when Dr. Goodman drafted the dispatch, I took it to "Brownie" (Lt. O. J. Brown), our communications officer, to send it to the Commander, Fleet Air Wing Three, signed by me as SENAV. The dispatch follows:

> DISPATCH: 19 JULY 1944 CONDITION OF SURVIVORS AS FOLLOWS X COFFIELD FRACTURED SKULL SEVERE LACERATIONS OF GROIN THIGHS SKULL FOREHEAD AND LEFT HAND SPRAINED RIGHT ANKLE X AINSCOUGH SEVERE MULTIPLE LACERATIONS OF HANDS FACE FOREHEAD THORAX BOTH LEGS X CUCCO FRACTURES LEFT FEMUR LACERATIONS OF FOREHEAD AND SKULL CONCUSSION OF BRAIN X SCHREINER LACERATIONS OF SKULL THORAX ABDOMEN HANDS CONTUSIONS OF PELVIS AND THORAX X DOCTOR SAYS ALL SURVIVORS CRITICALLY INJURED WITH POSSIBILITY OF INTERNAL INJURIES X PASS TO VICTOR PETER ONE FOR ACTION TO SECNAV IF APPROPRIATE FROM SENAV GALAPAGOS TO CFAW 3
>
> (S. C. Hair, Lieut (jg) A-V(N)
> Senior Naval Aviator)

As he proceeded with his ministrations to the injured, Dr. Goodman finally realized that the Navy had sent him to The Rock, possibly guided by divine intervention, so that he could meet the ultimate challenge—saving lives by using his full surgical skills so arduously learned at Columbia P & S. He now felt that, as a doctor, he was doing something important for the war effort and if it happened to be in the Galapagos Islands, that was all right. He might have preferred a combat area, but there he might not have had time to do his watercolor sketches of the island scenery.

For about a week, he did not leave the dispensary. He set up a cot and slept there all night every night, getting up every few hours to inspect the four patients. It is probable they might not have lived otherwise. If he hadn't been there, in my uneducated medical opinion, they would have died. After about ten days of treatment, the four patients were able to come out to rest on the concrete porch of the dispensary for a couple of hours each day, to be in the therapeutic atmosphere of bright sun and clean air.

Cucco, the machinist's mate, was an excitable Italian and the most vociferous in the group.

"I was a dead son of a bitch," he would say with great feeling, "but here I am now. Thank you, God, and thank you Dr. Goodman!" the other three were glad he said it because they felt the same way.

They made enough progress to be flown first to the Navy hospital in Coco Solo and then to the Corpus Christie Naval Air Station hospital. Coffield elected to keep on flying and recovered enough to join another squadron of multi-engine P2V patrol planes out of Norfolk. The three enlisted men chose to go home with honorable medical discharges. Because the episode involved no enemy action, they received no medals.

In our squadron, as in all squadrons in wartime, there was a strong sense of camaraderie.

The senior pilots never segregated themselves from the rest of us. We had a lot of respect for them, and if given a choice, preferred to fly with them. "Judge" Cauthan (so-called because his father was a superior court judge in Texas) was one of that group and we could not understand why, with all his experience, he would choose to ignore the orthodox and accepted landing technique for these large, multi-engine flying boats and kill himself and four others by making a downwind power landing. Our skipper got all of us pilots together at a morning muster, sat us down in the dining hall and gave us a lecture on what we already knew but needed to be reminded of; don't cowboy these airplanes but land them according to the accepted procedure.

Dr. Goodman

A LONG GOODBYE

In August 1944, a dispatch came from COMAIRLANT (Commander Air Force Atlantic Fleet) to COMFAIRWINGTHREE (Commander Fleet Air Wing Three) outlining "turn-in and replacement schedules" for our Coronado PB2Y-3 aircraft by the last quarter of that year. All the planes were to be returned to San Diego beginning August 15. The squadron was decommissioned at the end of December 1944.

I made the first such trip returning a plane to San Diego in early October. We flew from Corinto to Corpus Christie, Texas, an eight hour trip, on October 2nd. Bad weather delayed us two days so we completed our overland flight of nine and one-half hours on October 5.

Beginning October 6, I had twenty days leave. In the Navy in World War II, if you were a pilot, you could get a ride to anywhere in the United States, or even in the free world if you wanted to travel light and wait around in various naval air stations or stops on the schedules of the Naval Air Transport Service (NATS). I was able to get on NATS flights from San Diego to Asheville, North Carolina, then took a short train ride to Tryon, North Carolina, to visit Carter Brown at his resort hotel there, the Pine Crest Inn. His season at Castle Park ended September 30 so he was in Tryon until May. I was a sort of honored guest (at a reduced rate) in the small town in the "thermal belt" of the Blue Ridge Mountains. I joined two lady guests in extensive horseback rides almost every morning. Their husbands were still overseas in the Army. Evenings I was an invited guest to the homes of some old family friends from Chicago and Castle Park, now retired and living in Tryon.

When the time came, I left Tryon on a train for Atlanta and NATS flights to Miami and Coco Solo. I was back on duty as a pilot October 28, flying from Coco Solo to The Rock. We had routine patrol duty with our remaining airplanes for two more months.

My second trip to San Diego, and my last flight out of The Rock, was January 8, 1945, when our squadron was finally leaving after one year. The ferry route for all our planes back to San Diego was determined for us without any options. We were to fly from The Rock to Coco Solo, Key West, Corpus Christie, Salton Sea, and San Diego. My flight took nine days. This was mostly due to weather delays at Key West and Corpus Christie. We had to fly strictly VFR (Visual Flight Rules), carefully maneuvering at about 8,000 feet between some of the higher peaks in our flight path through Arizona. Flying boats can land only on bodies of water large enough to permit not only a landing, but a takeoff requiring about two miles of water. We had no alternate landing areas on this overland part of the trip, so we had to hope for no engine failure before we got to Salton Sea, our refueling stop before going over the Sierras to San Diego.

Our squadron was now decommissioned and The Rock was left to the flightless cormorants, the giant tortoises, the blue-footed boobies and all the other indigenous creatures. We were to leave it unmolested by humankind, except for our own temporary military installation, just as it had been for many thousands of years. We did change it by putting several hundred people there for four years, but in 1946, the navy CB's took down most of the salvageable buildings and sent them with other remaining equipment back to Panama. A few Ecuadorian police remained as caretakers. I feel no need to go back, but will remember it as it was. My log book shows that my first trip to The Rock was January 24, 1944, and my final departure was January 8, 1945. In that year's time, I recorded thirty-one round trips between The rock and Corinto, and two round trips each to Salinas, Ecuador, and Tulare, Peru. Each one-way flight averaged about nine hours.

EPILOGUE

Fred Coffield, the only pilot to survive the plane crash at The Rock, was my long-time friend. We had not been to the same flight school but had been assigned to VP-1 at Norfolk and went together to join the squadron at Coco Solo in April 1943. We were both from the Midwest, he from South Bend, I from Chicago. He had played football at Wabash College. We both shared a skeptical view of many aspects of Navy orthodoxy. Fred was fun-loving, handsome, had a wild sense of humor, and was attractive to women. We shared many experiences in the fleshpots of Colon, including several all-night wanderings among various night clubs and bars.

Over the years, we kept up with each other's whereabouts and jobs. Fred moved from South Bend to Richmond where he became a prosperous real estate operator and raised a large family. We carried on considerable correspondence for many years, at least partly because he was dedicated politically to the far fight of the Republican Party and he attempted, with evangelical fervor to convert me to the True Faith of Oliver North and Ronald Reagan. I was able to remain an unreconstructed, unredeemed liberal Democrat and he finally lost all hope for me.

Dr. Goodman, with the decommissioning of our squadron, was assigned to a Naval Hospital in Norfolk and returned to New York at the war's end. He married soon after that and embarked on a highly successful career as a surgeon in Manhattan. He and his wife Marian raised two daughters, and Marian became an accomplished watercolor artist, doing mostly marine scenes in the Scottish out-islands. After a long and active practice, Dr Goodman retired to Sands Point, Long Island, where he perfected his golf game and did some independent research.

Every year for fifty-four years on July 17, Fred Coffield sent a telegram to Dr. Goodman saying, "Dear Ed, Thank you for another year of my life." In the 1990s, Fred began to suffer a long, undiagnosed, debilitating illness possibly as a result of complications caused by the plane crash, but ultimately recognized as ALS, or Lou Gehrig's Disease. He was treated by several different clinics including Mayo's and Hopkins', but finally died in November 1998.

Dr. Goodman outlived his patient. I received a letter from him after Fred passed away.

Dear Sam,

I was grieved to learn about Fred, especially how he died. I sent his son a copy of the sketch I did of him the night of the accident. Marian is returning today. She spent two weeks in Skye, Scotland. Wendy, our oldest daughter, was with her. Come see us. I'm 91 years old.

–Ed

AFTER THE ROCK

Our January 1945 flight from The Rock to San Diego, via NAS Corpus Christie, was to deliver the last of our PB2Y Coronado four-engine seaplanes back to Consolidated Aircraft. There is only one PB2Y surviving after all these years; it is on display as a WWII relic in the Naval Aviation Museum at Pensacola.

We were given ten days leave and new orders. My orders were to the Multi-engine Instrument Instructors' School in Florida at Jacksonville NAS. This was a two-month course in Twin-Beech aircraft. They assumed that my previous instrument experience was irrelevant; we had to fly patterns "under the hood", with tolerances of five knots of airspeed, fifty feet of altitude, and three degrees of compass heading. We attended classes where we were endlessly lectured on such arcane subjects as "The Aerodynamics Of The Turn", and in which we found it difficult to stay awake. At the end, I was given a framed certificate saying I was now a "Multi-Engine Instrument Instructor". I am thankful that I never became one.

My next orders came in April to report to the Naval Air Navigation School at NAS Clinton, Oklahoma, to fly the R4D-7, the Navy version of the DC-3, a wonderful airplane. I did not know where Clinton was, but I knew about where Oklahoma was. So, I bought a 1939 two-door Studebaker Champion at a Jacksonville used-car lot, my first car in fourteen years, and set out for Indian Territory. I went in a northwesterly direction, stopping at two-dollar tourist camps, and going through a flood in Arkansas to reach highway 66 at Little Rock; then west to Oklahoma and Clinton. When I got to the town of Clinton, the NAS wasn't there; it was at Burns Flat, about fifteen miles further on highway 66, then south a few miles on highway 183.

I had been given what the Navy thought was a good, easy assignment. Pan American Airways had earlier given up the dubious job of training Navy air navigators, and tossed its navigation school back into the Navy's lap. This led to the establishment in the Oklahoma back-country of the Naval Air Navigation Squadron—NANS. I was one of the 42 pilots assigned to flying the students around the surrounding countryside, including the adjoining states, while they practiced air navigation. Our flights lasted about four hours; each plane was fitted out with desks for sixteen student navigators. Occasionally, we would have to fly through a thunderhead to stay on course, and the students would be bounced around and become navigationally disoriented. Fortunately, during the several months we were doing this, I never once got lost, mostly because in the West, the railroads, highways, and section lines are all visible and straight to each of the four cardinal compass points. The sun also rises and sets in the usual directions. Sometimes, the students were heard to say things like what Dorothy said: "Toto, I don't think we're in Kansas any more . . . " I also realized that to get lost with sixteen navigators on board would be more than ironic; the Navy could not survive.

As the summer passed and VJ day came, NANS was decommissioned, the Naval Air Station became a stop on the Transcontinental Naval Air Transport Service. They needed a few senior pilots, so I stayed until the end of the year.

VI. FINIS ORIGINE PENDET

OUT OF UNIFORM

In December, I drove to Memphis to the Naval Air Station there to be mustered out of the Navy, and sent back to civilian life after four years. The Navy required a home address, but I didn't have one, so I had them ship my sea chest to my sister in Waterville, Maine. I asked her to keep it for me until I settled somewhere. My parents had retired to Tryon, North Carolina, but I had no thought of living there permanently. I thought, of course, I'll return to Chicago, find a place to live, and get a job.

I ended up in an apartment on Greenwood Avenue in Hyde Park near the university—the neighborhood where I had spent my life before the Navy. With the help of some friends in the advertising business, I became gainfully employed by a Chicago division of the Borden Company, editing and producing two internal house organs. A year later, I moved to United Airlines, in charge of newspaper advertising.

On a vacation from my job in 1947, I visited my parents in Tryon, North Carolina, still undetermined as to where I really wanted to be. I had seen much of the North Carolina "thermal belt" on previous visits to Carter Brown at The Pine Crest Inn in Tryon over the years. I knew about the area's salubrious climate, enabling my father to play golf all winter, if he wanted to. I also knew about Chicago winters, with the cold, damp wind off the lake, and snow that fell and then got dirty, and finally melted. North Carolina had many inviting features which attracted me. Charlotte and the Piedmont area between the mountains and the shore were rapidly growing. I made a quick trip back to Chicago, said goodbye to United Airlines, put my worldly goods into my Ford sedan, and drove to North Carolina and Charlotte. Typical of those progressive business times in the Carolinas, Piedmont Airlines was being formed in Winston-Salem; I went to work for the Charlotte advertising agency that had the account.

FINALLY . . .

In 1949 after three years of persuasion I succeeded in my single-minded selling job of persuading Elisabeth Cox Green that we should be married. The ceremony was in June at the First Presbyterian Church in St Louis. She brought with her Camilla, her three-year-old daughter, a delightful, affectionate, helpful child, who, in a way, made up for my lost time. I was 34 years old. I now felt that I had my own family. By 1950, Camilla had a sister, Stephanie; by 1954, another sister, Elisabeth; and by 1956, another sister, Julie. Her sisters very early came to the conclusion that Camilla is the one to go to if you have a problem that you don't want to tell your mother about. We now have four sons-in-law, and six grandchildren. When we were first married, Camilla called me "Sam"; then, after a couple of months, she began to call me "Daddy". This gave me great satisfaction. Over the years, Liz became active in local Democratic politics, and was the first woman to be elected chairman of the Mecklenburg County Commission, where she served eight years. She came to my rescue by marrying me soon enough to save me from the stubborn and unhealthy habits of bachelorhood which were taking me in meaningless directions. I have been grateful ever since.

While in St Louis prior to our wedding day, I learned that in the 1940s whose who lived west of the Mississippi were not sure where Charlotte was. There was a general perception that it could be in Virginia, West Virginia, or South Carolina; each of those states had cities with names that sounded like Charlotte. Liz's mother gave her some last-minute instructions after the wedding, before her only daughter went off to live in terra incognita:

"Don't ever learn to iron . . . And you will need mosquito-netting to put around your bed."

During her subsequent visits to Charlotte, my mother-in-law found that Charlotte was indeed becoming civilized and had some nice neighborhoods. We who have lived in Charlotte for many years know that our quality of life has attracted several hundred thousand new residents since our early married years.

I BECOME AN ENTREPRENEUR

In 1952 I put together an outdoor advertising company. This was an adventure that lasted thirty-five years, and that gave me a great appreciation for the American entrepreneurial ways of doing business in a city that was friendly to such enterprises. There were some dismaying episodes: One such was when the president of the Charlotte Chamber Of Commerce appeared at a City Council meeting, and demanded legislation to eliminate all outdoor advertising billboards in the city. I had served for several years on the aviation committee of the Chamber, so I couldn't quite figure out why they now wanted to put me out of business. Fortunately, our friends on the council prevailed and nothing happened.

In 1987 I sold our company to a larger regional outdoor advertising business, and I was free again, as I had been in 1945 on being mustered out of the Navy. I no longer had to listen to the observations of some of my friends who accused me of ruining the scenery with billboards. I did not admit to that; I do admit to sharing some of that responsibility with other legitimate roadside businesses.

POLITICAL MATURITY

Just as in our family the Presbyterian Church was the only True church, so the Republican Party was our protector against the strange and suspicious objectives of the Democrats.

My one and only departure from this mind-set was in 1937, when in graduate school at the university I joined a group not only liberal but part of the Communist apparatus of that time, the American Student Union Against War & Fascism, or the ASU. A cell was formed with the purpose of joining with the Russians in their support of the *Republic* in the Spanish Civil War, and opposing the *Nationalists*, supported by the Germans. I paid dues, we had meetings, and at least two of our members went to Spain to join the Abraham Lincoln Brigade. This was my only departure from Republican orthodoxy.

After a couple of years in Charlotte, and after marrying a wife who was not only politically motivated but active in the local Democratic organization, I began to think deep thoughts about the sagacity of the Truman administration, and my admiration for "the man from Missouri." At that time in North Carolina the Republican Party was almost inconsequential. If one wanted to be politically active, in most elections the Democrats fielded the winning candidates, and had by far the dominant local organizations. My apostasy was complete when I registered as a Democrat, and voted for Adlai Stevenson in 1952. I was careful not to discuss this with my father.

I'M INTERVIEWED BY A GRANDSON

In later years, one of our grandsons, John Cummings Divine, age 12, was assigned by his Social Studies teacher to interview a veteran of WWII. The veteran easiest for him to find was his grandfather, so he came over to see me, bringing his tape recorder, and we talked about the war that had ended 56 years previously.

EXCERPTS:

Q. How did the war affect you and your family?

A. Pearl Harbor had the effect of uniting everybody in the United States, with the objective of defeating the Japanese and the Germans. There were certain changes in our lives, such as gasoline rationing. Other things were unavailable, including canned goods and other items in the grocery stores. but mostly, the whole country was dedicated to the war.

Q. When did you first start to hear news reports and understand what Hitler was doing to the Jews?

A. I think the first time I ever heard about it was late in the war, perhaps in 1943, when it became apparent what was happening over there; it was hard for people outside of Germany to find out about it and to realize the enormity of what was happening.

Q. What did you think at the time about the dropping of the atomic bombs to end the war?

A. I thought that it need not be done at the time. Later, General Eisenhower said that the atomic bomb need not have been used because by that time the Japanese had no air force and no navy. But the atomic bomb program had a certain momentum going, and President Truman decided to use it.

Q. What do you think about the dropping of the atomic bombs to end the war now?

A. I keep being told that it saved a lot of American lives. I'm not sure that conventional carpet bombing of the Japanese cities would not have done the same thing; I'm not sure anybody else knows.

Q. What else would you like to tell my social studies class about WWII?

A. Well, I would say that WWII was such a catastrophe that it's unimaginable. We lost in one morning at Pearl Harbor more men than were killed in our army in France in World War I; plus our casualties at Omaha Beach, plus the refusal of the Japanese to surrender and our great casualties in the Pacific islands, plus the Russian war against the Germans where in one winter it was possible for a million men to be killed, plus the dreadful siege at Stalingrad, plus our inexcusable bombing of Dresden, all these describe only a part of WWII. We also need to remember that the whole German nation was dedicated to the extermination of innocent unarmed people. Hitler turned his own countrymen into savage beasts.

Q. Did you want to go to the war?

A. It wasn't a question of wanting to go to war. I knew I was the right age, I had no obligation not to go; I had no necessary civilian experience, so I knew I was going. But so did everybody else my age that I knew. So, it's sort of an unanswerable question. We knew we had to go, so we went anyway.

Q. What was the worst thing about the war, to you?

A. Our squadron didn't see any combat, but I had some anxious moments flying through hurricanes as a part of our designated patrols. World War II was the United Stated Navy's finest hour. We were proud to be in it. If there was a best thing about the war to me, that was it. Our squadron was given a job to do, and we did it. But in retrospect, looking back on WWII, it was a catastrophe the like of which was never seen in the ancient world or in the modern world. It was a war we had to win, but at an enormous cost.

BACK TO THE CASTLE

In March 1975 I wrote to Carter Brown at Castle Park, where he now lived the year round, telling him of the death of my mother in Tryon, North Carolina. He wrote back, saying:

> *Marion and I send our deepest sympathies when an old timer Castle Parker such as your mother, leaves us. Your father was also a true Castle Parker. . . . I know you will keep your memories of childhood in Castle Park and the freedom that was so much a part of your early years before the 'play class'. Marion sends her love. Carter B.*

In October, I wrote Carter telling him of my upcoming trip to Chicago, where I would spend two days, then come to Castle Park for two days. I would stay at a hotel in Macatawa. Carter wrote back and invited me to stay with him and Marion; they were now permanently located in a house they had built in a newly-landscaped area deep in the trees behind the Castle. They were there with two servants who had been with them in Tryon for many years.

October can be pleasant in lower western Michigan, and so it was during my visit. I was free to hike to Macatawa and various other places that brought back childhood memories. There were still several occupied cottages, so I visited a few where there were those who might remember me. Long conversations with Carter and Marion filled me in with reports of events and people in recent years.

This was my last extended visit to Castle Park. Some previous visits had been after WWII and before I moved to North Carolina. I knew only a few of the members of the remaining families. My father sold our cottage in 1958 to a family from St Louis, who had been renting it for parts of several summers. It has now been remodeled and "winterized," with new plumbing, a new kitchen, HVAC, telephone and television.

Most of the former "summer cottages" at Castle Park have been replaced or converted to year-round use, some quite upscale. Castle Park mothers no longer cook on kerosene stoves. The golf course with its sand greens and clay tees is gone, replaced by landscaped greensward where the unkempt fairways were. There are no horses in the stable down below the Castle. No longer is ice cut from Kelly Lake in the winter to supply the Castle Park iceboxes in the summer. "The Shack" for the waiters is gone. The beach has been gone since the 1950's when Lake Michigan rose a few inches, enough to eliminate a 150 feet of clean sandy waterfront.

But Castle Park is alive and well. It is still a haven for families from the Middle West, some of them the third and fourth generations. There is an increasing number of families from Grand Rapids. As a substitute for the beach, there is an Olympic swimming pool on the campus where the eighth golf fairway was. There are several all-weather new tennis courts. On the dune next to the lake, there is a clubhouse for meetings and social events.

Three years after my visit a letter came, October 18, 1978, from Ken Ratcliffe at Castle Park. He was a long-time friend from Chicago and a second-generation cottage owner:

Dear Sam:
We are here for the month of October. Just a note to say that Carter Brown died early this morning. He was 85. It was his wish that there be no funeral or memorial service. He is to be cremated and the ashes scattered on top of Baldy. Marion asked me to let you know.
We know how much he gave to Castle Park, so it's a great loss. We send our best to you.

Ken

∼

Baseball is still being played at Castle Park, but without Carter Brown, seated at his usual place near first base, the most vocal one in the gallery, exhorting us to victory in our monthly seven-inning softball games with the boys from Ottawa Beach in the 1920's. When we were in the field, outscored and outplayed, making our usual errors, he would stand up, wave his fist at us, and shout, "You're playing blase baseball!" He would repeat this throughout the game, sometimes alternating with another admonition, "Come on, boys! This is BASEBALL! Not a picnic!" Usually we lost, but no matter what the outcome, when it was over he would leave us with, "OKAY, OKAY! Great game boys!"

As Satchel Paige once said, "The past is a long and twisty road...." And so it is that, sometimes, swimming around in my head are persistent fragments of old songs, coming back to me without any effort to recall them. I hear the melodies of "Whispering", and "Swingin' Down The Lane", which I must have heard while sitting behind the piano at the Castle Park dances.

AUTHOR'S NOTE Some parts of my stories may be unintentionally fictionalized, due to the passage of six of seven decades, and the consequent dimming of certain memories. but I've retrieved them as best I can, with no intentional embellishment.

Sam Hair is a native of Chicago and a graduate of the University of Chicago. He has been a ranger in Rocky Mountain National Park, a Naval Aviator in World War II in the Atlantic and Pacific theaters, and an entrepreneur businessman in Charlotte, North Carolina for thirty-seven years. His wife Elisabeth is a native of St. Louis, a graduate of Wellesley College, and a local elected political office holder. They have four daughters, six grandchildren, and recently celebrated their fiftieth anniversary. Hair is now active in the commercial real estate business in Charlotte and pursues his interests in photography and tennis.